BLACK MINISTERS AND LAITY IN THE URBAN CHURCH

An Analysis of Political and Social Expectations

James H. Harris

UNIVERSITY PRESS OF AMERICA

LANHAM • NEW YORK • LONDON

Library of Congress Cataloging in Publication Data

Harris, James H., 1952-
   Black ministers and laity in the urban church.

   Bibliography: p.
   Includes index.
   1. Afro-American churches.   2. Afro-American
clergy.   3. Laity.   I. Title.
   BR563.N4B575   1987   253'.2'08996073   86-28151
   ISBN 0-8191-5823-2 (alk. paper)
   ISBN 0-8191-5824-0 (pbk. : alk. paper)

Dedication

To my wife, Demetrius Dianetta and my sons,
James Corey-Alexander and Cameron Christopher-David,
and to my parents Richard and Carrie Anna Harris

Acknowledgements

This book was made possible with the continued support of the Mount Pleasant Baptist Church and the willingness of several ministers to allow me access to their congregations. Without their support, this work would have been virtually impossible.

Several professors at Old Dominion University must be acknowledged for their helpful involvement throughout the initial process. Kato B. Keeton, Ph.D. was the dissertation director and extremely helpful throughout the process. To her, I am eternally grateful for the suggestions and encouragement which enabled me to complete the initial work. Maurice R. Berube, Ph.D., and Leonard Ruchelman, Ph.D. evaluated the initial manuscript.

Also appreciated were the efforts of Patricia Dandridge, Demetrius Alexander, Cecelia Frazier, Dawn Stubbs, Lydia Whittaker, Stanley Osborne, Jr., Myrna Whittaker and Lisa Tyson who served as survey assistants. Additionally, Dr. Charles F. Abel of the University of Northern Illinois, was very helpful at a critical time, Dr. Jack Robinson of Old Dominion University, Dr. King E. Davis of Virginia Commonwealth University, Dr. William Gibson, University of the Redlands, and Dr. Harold E. Braxton, Virginia State University, offered invaluable assistance during different stages of the development of this book. Mrs. Evangeline Buggs has typed and retyped this manuscript with extreme meticulousness and care. To her, I am very thankful.

I am extremely indebted to the book *Ministry In America* and its authors David Schuller, Merton Strommen and Milo Brekke. Their work inspired me and enabled me to develop the initial prospectus. Additionally, I have not only drawn extensively from the aforesaid book, but also from *Readiness for Ministry*, Vols. 1 and 2. The Association of Theological Schools in America and Canada has generously granted permission to use some important material without which this book would not have been possible. Additionally, the Council on Interracial Books for Children has allowed us to use data from their publication, *Fact Sheet on Institutional Racism, 1985.* I am very thankful for their generosity.

My family has always supported my efforts. Therefore, without the encouragement and inspiration of my wife, Demetrius, and my sons, James Corey-Alexander and Cameron Christopher-David the completion of this book would have been prohibited. To them, I express my thankfulness for being there all the time, especially in my most difficult moments.

Although many persons helped in the development of my thoughts, I am solely responsible for any lack of clarity or other shortcomings of this book.

Table of Contents

ACKNOWLEDGEMENTS v

LIST OF TABLES ix

LIST OF FIGURES xi

CHAPTER

    I. The Black Urban Church: Clergy and Laity 1

    II. What the Laity Expect of the Minister 9

    III. Ambivalence Among Minister and Laity 51

    IV. Implications of What the Laity Expect 65

    V. An Essay on Sources 75

BIBLIOGRAPHY 97

APPENDICES 105

List of Tables

Table

1. Demographic Characteristics of the Respondents 11

2. Aggressive Political Leadership 13

3. Active Concern for the Oppressed 14

4. Precedence of Evangelistic Goals 15

5. Percentage of Responses to: Participates in an Effort to Remove an Incompetent or Ineffective Official from School 17

6. Percentage of Responses to: Speaks from the Pulpit about Political Issues 18

7. Percentage of Responses to: Uses Principles and Methods of Social Organization for Political Change 19

8. Percentage of Responses to: Organizes Groups to Change Civil Laws Which Seem in Light of Scripture to be Morally Wrong 20

9. Percentage of Responses to: Encourages Non-Union Laborers to Organize 21

10. Percentage of Responses to: Is Willing to Risk Arrests to Protests Social Wrongs 22

11. Percentage of Responses to: Works to Make Sure that all People are Free to Buy Property in Areas of Their Choice 23

12. Percentage of Responses to: Pressures Public Officials
on Behalf of the Oppressed 24

13. Percentage of Responses to: Organizes Action
Groups in the Congregation to Accomplish
Directly Some Political Goal 25

14. Percentage of Responses to: Organizes Study
Groups To Discuss Public Affairs 26

15. Percentage of Responses to: Declares a Willingness
to Run for Public Office in the Community 28

16. Percentage of Responses to: Takes an Informed
Position on Controversial Community Issues 29

17. Percentage of Responses to: Works Toward Racial
Integration in the Community 31

18. Percentage of Responses to: Uses Authoritative
Information and Facts to Meet Racism and
Prejudice 32

19. Percentage of Responses to: Works to Integrate
People of Varying Educational, Ethnic and
Cultural Background 34

20. Percentage of Responses to: Acquaints Self with the
History and Aspirations of Minority Groups and
Other Oppressed People 36

21. Percentage of Responses to: Makes Individuals
Aware of Their Possible Part in Causing World
Poverty 36

22. Percentage of Responses to: Recommends That the
Parish Cut Off Financial Support for Institutions
that Discriminate 38

23. Percentage of Responses to: Holds That the
Church's Task of Proclaiming the Gospel by
Preaching and Teaching Overshadow . . . Helping
to Eliminate Suffering 40

24. Percentage of Responses to: Frequently
Approaches Strangers to Ask About the
Condition of Their Souls 41

25. Percentage of Responses to: The Way to Build An
Ideal World Society is to Convert Everyone to
Christianity 42

26. Percentage of Responses to: Insists that Clergy
Should Stick to Religion and not be Concerned
with . . . Political Questions 43

27. Relationship of Denomination and Responses to:
Organizes Groups to Change Civil Laws which
Seems in the Light of Scripture to be Morally
Wrong 115

28. Relationship of Denomination and Responses to:
Works to Integrate People of Varying Educational,
Ethnic, and Cultural Backgrounds 116

29. Relationship of Denomination and Responses to:
Holds that the Church's Task of Proclaiming the
Gospel by Preaching and Teaching Overshadows
in Importance the Task of Helping to Eliminate 117

30. Relationship of Education and Responses to:
Prioritizes in Use of Time Indicate the Belief that
the One and Only Way to Build an Ideal World
Society is to Convert Everyone 118

31. Relationship of Income and Responses to: Priorities
in Use of Time 119

32. Relationship of Occupation and Response to:
Works to Integrate People 120

33. Relationship of Occupation and Response to:
Acquaints Self with 121

List of Figures

Figure

1. Mean Level of Importance by Cluster ....

Chapter One

The Black Urban Church: Clergy and Laity

*"Except the Lord Keep the city, the
watchman waketh but in vain"
(Psalm 127:16)*

Historical Overview

The Black church in America began in the hearts and souls of
Afro-American slaves who had been uprooted and transported to
the United States to be auctioned to the highest bidder. As chattel
property, these Black people had been legally and socially violated to
the extent that their ontological status was essentially denied. Their
humanness was rejected by the nature and spirit of law and social
structure. This was indeed the most serious effect of slavery because
as an institution, slavery tended to negate Descartes' maxim, "cogito
ergo sum." However, this attempt at total emasculation—a delib-
erate effort to strip the Black American of any vestige of honor and
respect, failed from the beginning. Much of this failure can be
attributed to the inner ability of Blacks to survive in the midst of
extremely difficult situations. The journey to America, aboard the
slave ships was a cruel oddyssey to a land where oppression would
be perpetuated. Nevertheless, those who survived, had to have been
physically tough and spiritually determined.

So the slaves' inner strength and stamina vis-a-vis the teaching
and evangelization efforts of the Quakers helped to enable the Black

church to begin. Carter G. Woodson states that:

> The real interest in the evangelization of the negroes
> in the English Colonies . . . was manifested by the
> Quakers. . . . In accepting these persons of color
> on a basis of religious equality and denouncing the
> nakedness of the religions of the other colonists at
> the same time, the Quakers alienated their affection
> and easily brought down upon them the wrath of the
> public functionaries in these plantations.[1]

The white slaveholders did not want the slaves to read, write or be taught the ways of self-determination because they felt that non-beings should not be accorded such rights. In spite of this, "George Fox was advocating the instruction of Negroes in 1672 and in 1679 boldly entreating his co-workers to instruct and teach the Indians and Negroes how 'Christ by the grace of God had tasted death for every man.' "[2] The evangelization effort by the Quakers provided the foundation for the slaves to assert their own humanity in later years. Moreover, as time elapsed and Christianity became more under-stood, slaves began to draw inferences and make deductions from their experiences. Religious equality advocated by the Quakers was not compatible with social, economic, political and humanitarian inequality advocated and perpetuated by law and public policy. This dilemma or contradiction was recognized and repelled by the slaves who witnessed America's resolve to be free from the oppressive power of England while simultaneously subjugating them and violating their human rights. "As early as 1774 American slaves were declaring publicly and politically that they thought Christianity and slavery were incompatible."[3] This means that the Black church was born in the midst of a political struggle. Whites were struggling for their freedom from their mother country and Blacks were enslaved struggling to be free in America. This paradoxical situation repre-sented the embodiment of contradiction and oppression. During these early years the Black church was formed and shaped by the experiences of degradation, despair and disgrace vis-a-vis a desire to be free. Leroy Fitts indicates that:

> During the formative period of Black Church life, the
> Black Baptist Preachers, more specifically had to
> come to grips with the pragmatic situation of life in

America. They had to relate a relevant theology to slavery in the South and White racism throughout the nation. They had to keep in tune with the heartbeats of their brothers in Black.[4]

The minister and laity have historically been reflections of each other; however, the minister's commitment to preaching required a level of boldness that all were not endowed with. As a preacher, the minister was a leader that enabled others to understand the socio-political and theological dimensions of life. "The Black Baptist Preachers were, in a real sense, the political and social philosophers of the race. They were able and fearless advocates of truth, justice and equal rights for an oppressed people."[5]

The Black church was born during slavery and continued to grow and thrive throughout each phase of American history. Today, it is a strong institution consisting of several national conventions and millions of constituents. The laity in these churches possess a strong numerical presence and power that is capable of changing the face of urban America. The Black church is a social institution as Kenneth Clark and others have described; however, it is also the harborer of tremendous political strength that is increasingly becoming more apparent via the laity. The laity have become more educated and economically stable. Their ranks include professionals from every major field of expertise, i.e., medicine, law, business, humanities, social science, and engineering. The constituents of the Black urban church have survived many hardships and difficulties, and these experiences have contributed to their stamina and strength.

The Black laity constitute a relatively stable, captive audience that can influence the political and socio-economic agenda of the minister if he is aware of their expectations. This is not to suggest that ministers will or should adhere to the wishes and wants of the laity; rather to indicate that the writer sought a description and analysis of expectations of ministers particularly concerning political and socio-economic issues or problems in the urban environment. Therefore, the purpose here was to ascertain information regarding the laity's expectations of the Black minister in terms of his political and socio-economic involvement in the urban condition. More precisely, answers were sought to the questions: Do the persons who attend the Black church expect the minister to deal with socio-economic and political problems? What particular urban problems do they expect him or her to offer leadership in facing or solving? It is assumed that persons who attend church are interested in spiritual growth of some sort? Given this assumption, the writer sought to determine what more do the Black laity expect other than spiritual leadership from the minister.

Distinction was made between denominations or types of churches because the city has a sufficient number of Black Protestant denominations as well as other forms of Christian churches to merit a meaningful contrast in points of view regarding their expectations. The use of the term "Black urban church laity" will refer to all of those denominations or sects that constitute organized Black religious bodies.

The minister and laity are inextricably tied. Their relationship is akin to a doctor's relationship to patients or a teacher's relationship to students. More precisely, there is a mutual relationship such that each group needs the other in order to function as an effective group. Simultaneously, there is a chasm between the two as implied by the perceived dichotomy of classification.

The laity are an important, powerful group representing the essence of power in Congregational Churches as well as a growing force in the hierarchical churches. In autonomous churches or churches with congregational polity, the laity are the ultimate decision making body. Their expectations of the minister in dealing with the community and world (i.e., political and social problems) will provide the minister with guidance in meeting the needs of his/her congregation and the larger urban community.

Expectations of the laity concerning the minister's involvement in political and socio-economic problems in the urban community may help to develop a mechanism for addressing some of the prevailing issues in an urban area. Moreover, the *a priori* assumption that undergirds this rationale implies that as responsible, social and political beings, ministers will adapt to the level of expectations displayed on the part of the laity if these expectations do not morally and ethically diminish his character. This adaptation is a positive sign of the minister's capacity to be flexible in situations that demand pliability rather than excessive dogmatism.

The Black church is an intricate part of the urban community in America. Moreover, it is also the most independent, self-determining institution in the Black community. Each person who participates in the church, however marginally, and is not a licensed or ordained minister constitutes the laity. Much has been written about the leadership in the Black community recognizing that the church has been a forerunner in developing said leaders—especially the clergy. Conversely, very few have focused mainly upon the laity's expectations of the leaders. Dubose writes,

> As Blacks became urbanized, they became better educated. They produced outstanding leaders. Out of Black ghettos of America have come some of the leading citizens in education, politics, sports, and entertainment. The church has been prominent in developing these leaders. The Black pastor today enjoys a much higher community status than his White counterpart.[6]

Because the Black minister serves a people who have historically been victimized by institutional oppression, injustice, and racism, it is important to understand the expectations of the laity in urban areas in order to chart the future directions of the minister as he serves the urban community.

A look at expectations of laity is timely and relates to a critical segment of the population because the Black church laity have the potential to help determine and shape the agenda and political involvement of the minister. Furthermore, there is a paucity of data on laity expectations that focus exclusively upon the Black minister as a leader in an urban setting.

Moreover, the urban minister and laity are surrounded by a variety of political and social conditions of poverty, racism, injustice and oppression that are endemic to their existential situation. In order for the minister not to be supinely oblivious to these conditions, the laity's expectations can serve to foster a more active role in effectuating change or at least confronting the problems of the urban community.

Timeliness was augmented by the presidential candidacy of The Reverend Jesse Jackson who was the first Black minister to seek the highest political office in the land. Other clergy of equal and less renown already occupy political office or are involved in an attempt to eradicate social and political hardships among urban Blacks.

Additionally, Black ministers have historically been involved in the social and political dimensions of the urban milieu. Persons such as Nat Turner and Gabriel Prosser—persons whose names are "buried forever under the debris of the citadel of slavery"[7] as well as modern leaders such as Adam Clayton Powell, Malcolm X, Martin Luther King, Andrew Young, William Gray, and Wyatt Tee Walker, Ralph Abernathy, Joseph Lowry, Leon Sullivan and Walter Fauntleroy have exemplified the fact that Black ministers are involved in the political and social life of urban America. The extent to which Black urban laity expect such involvement is largely the focus of this work.

The Role of the Black Minister and Laity

The minister is like no other professional. He is preacher, teacher, administrator, encourager, counselor, leader and friend to all types of individuals. In the book, *Ten Faces of Ministry*, Milo Brekke, Merton Strommen and Dorothy Williams describe the minister quite thoroughly. They state,

> Ministers occupy a peculiar and sensitive position; they are persons both more powerful and less powerful than others with similar education and social status. People feel free to admire them extravagantly and criticize them severely. A minister occupies a very public position, yet often shares people's most private thoughts and concerns.[8]

The Black minister is expected to be a spiritual leader with the attendant administrative responsibilities in the church. However, his role extends beyond the specific responsibilities of the church into the wider community. Moreover, there are those within the church who feel that the minister should devote his time and energy to evangelistic goals such that the gospel might be propagated and reflected in his activities. Other laity want the minister to be actively involved in the dismantling of oppressive social, economic and political forces. The minister understands that the laity have mixed feelings about his active involvement in "politics." Nevertheless, he is often compelled to participate in the political sphere of urban America in order to effectuate change.

Historically, the Black minister has had to play numerous roles in the community because he was more insulated from the power of retribution wielded by whites who vehemently disagreed with his efforts to liberate oppressed people. The autonomy of the Black church, especially the Baptist Church, remains one of its most powerful tools. Because the church operates independent of the white power structure, it is uniquely and strategically capable of positively impacting upon the urban condition.

The condition of Black America demands that the Black urban minister give direction to the empowerment of a people who have been victimized by the abuse of power in American society. This empowerment can be achieved through educating Blacks about the serious need to develop a strong family structure, a strong and viable church, and a pool of economic and political analysts to develop the most viable methods to enhance the position of Blacks in America.

The Black minister and the church are critical to the development of a just and fair society. Certainly, the gospel must be preached, but the minister also has the responsibility for helping to liberate Black people from the forces of oppression that pervade the cities and towns of this nation. The harnessing of the strengths of the Black minister and laity will take ingenuity, creativity and commitment to the cause of freedom and justice.

In the following chapters, we shall explore the subject of Black ministers and laity and determine more clearly why neither can afford to be passive in a society that is actively engaged in efforts to exacerbate the inequities and unfairness that are endemic to life in urban America.

FOOTNOTES

[1] Carter G. Woodson, *The History of the Negro Church*, pp. 14-15.

[2] *Ibid.*, p. 15.

[3] Albert J. Raboteau, *Slave Religion: The Invisible Institution in the Antebellum South* (New York: Oxford University Press, 1978), p. 290.

[4] Leroy Fitts, *A History of Black Baptists* (Nashville, Tenn.: Broadman Press, 1985), p. 222.

[5] *Ibid.*, p. 226.

[6] Milo Brekke, Merton Strommen and Dorothy Williams, *Ten Faces of Ministry* (Minneapolis: Augsburg Publishing House, 1979), p. 9.

[7] Francis M. Dubose, *How Churches Grow in an Urban World* (Nashville: Broadman Press, 1978), p. 81.

[8] Gayraud S. Wilmore, *Black Religion and Black Radicalism* (New York: Doubleday, 1973), p. 89.

Chapter Two

What the Laity Expect of the Minister

Introduction

In ascertaining the Black church laity's expectations of clergy in urban areas—specifically as they related to social and political issues, a survey consisting of sixty-three questions and statements was used in order to determine answers to the following questions: Do Black church laity expect the minister to deal with socio-economic and political problems in urban areas? and, What particular urban problems do the laity expect the minister to offer leadership in facing or solving? The focus of this chapter is to answer the aforesaid questions.

This chapter focuses upon only those statements that constitute three clusters that have been determined to address the social and political expectations as well as the traditional expectations of laity. The contrast between the social and political sphere of ministry and the traditional sphere is represented by the following clusters: Aggressive Political Leadership, Active Concern for the Oppressed, and Precedence of Evangelistic Goals.

Each cluster was formed after the statements were determined to constitute the said subgroups using the cluster analysis technique. This information, i.e., clusters and individual statements constituting the clusters, was provided by the national study conducted by the Association of Theological Schools in America and Canada which culminated in the book, *Ministry In America*. Because the writer does not utilize analysis of variance, the emphasis here is placed on the uniqueness of each individual statement within each cluster. Moreover, this limitation is justified by the fact that the writer is chiefly concerned with the social and political expectations of laity regarding clergy and does not attempt to duplicate, to any degree, the national study mentioned earlier. More specifically, the writer will describe the extent to which persons in the Black urban church expected the minister to participate in the social and political realities of the urban milieu. This chapter provides an explanation of the responses to each statement that constitute the heretofore mentioned clusters.

Statistically significant relationships between specific variables, measured at the .05 level, are discussed in order to test the hypothesis. The chi-square statistic was used to determine if there was a significant relationship between denomination affiliation and each of the items in the core clusters that are constitutive of independent variables. Moreover, chi-square was used to determine if the socio-economic status (e.g., income, education and occupation) of the respondents was statistically significant relative to the individual items that are constitutive of the relevant clusters.

Characteristics of Respondents

The survey utilized ten churches which represented seven different denominations. There was a total of three hundred and thirty-eight respondents. Of those who responded, two hundred and forty were females (71.3 percent) and ninety-seven were males (28.7 percent). The two largest percentages of persons who responded were Baptists who comprised 36.1 percent of the total sample and, the Church of God in Christ which consisted of 19.8 percent of the sample. The fact that the Black church constituents are mostly female and Baptist is no surprise. This suggests that the sample is representative and, therefore, represents a microcosm of the Black church today. Moreover, 95.9 percent of the respondents were Black while a negligible percentage of other races were represented. Also, 28.4 percent of the respondents had attended college while 21.3 percent had attended high school or trade school. Furthermore, 15.7

percent were college graduates (Table 1).

TABLE 1

**DEMOGRAPHIC CHARACTERISTICS
OF THE RESPONDENTS**

	Number of Respondents	Percentage
A. DENOMINATION		
African Methodist Episcopal (Zion)	32	9.5
Baptist	122	36.1
Church of God In Christ	67	19.8
Episcopal	33	9.8
Presbyterian	18	5.3
Lutheran	23	6.8
Disciples of Christ	43	12.7
TOTAL	338	100.0
B. SEX		
Male	97	28.7
Female	241	71.3
TOTAL	338	100.0
C. EDUCATION		
Eighth grade or less	8	2.4
Some High School or Trade School	36	10.7
High School or Trade School Graduate	72	21.3
Some College	96	28.4
College Graduate	53	15.7
Some Graduate or Professional	31	9.2
Seminary Graduate	1	.3
Masters	20	5.9
Masters plus	14	4.1
Doctorate	7	2.1
TOTAL	338	100.0
D. INCOME		
Under $3,000	20	5.9
$3,000 – $5,999	9	2.7
$6,000 – $8,999	15	4.4
$9,000 – $11,999	23	6.8
$12,000 – $14,999	38	11.2
$15,000 – $17,999	31	9.2
$18,000 – $20,999	30	8.9
$21,000 – $23,999	31	9.2
$24,000 – $26,999	29	8.6
$27,000 – and above	112	33.1
TOTAL	338	100.0

These statistics indicate that the Black urban church laity are becoming more educated. This indication corresponds with the general increase in the number and percentage of Blacks matriculating and graduating from colleges in the past twenty years.

> A study by the Center for the Study of Social Policy found that: Between 1960 and 1981 Black males made a gain of 4.4 years of schooling on the average, compared with 1.9 years for white males. By 1981, the median level of schooling for Black males and females was above 12 years, and the difference between White and Black years of schooling was only half a year.[1]

Although the percentage of Black college graduates has increased over the past fifteen years, it is much less than the 15.7 percent found in this study's sample.

> Census Bureau data show that in 1967, the year before the education push began, 6.8 percent of white adults and 2.6 percent of Black adults had graduated from college. Last year (1983) the figures were 11 percent of white adults and 5.7 percent of Black adults. . . .[2]

The percentage of college graduates was almost three times larger than the percentage of Black graduates in the general population.

Moreover, 33.1 percent of the respondents earned $27,000 or more while 11.2 percent earned $12,000 to $14,999. These data suggest that the sample was more economically advantaged than the general Black population.

The rate of poverty among Blacks in the South and the nation is increasing at an alarming rate.

In December of 1984, Steve Suitts prepared a report for the Southern Regional Council which stated,

> Some groups have been particularly affected by the steady increases in the poverty rate in both the South and the nation since 1979. Including more than 1 in 3 Blacks, the nation's poverty rate of 35.7 percent for all Black persons rose in the last four years from 31 percent in 1979. Not since 1968 has the poverty rate

for Blacks reached such a high level. While the exact
statistical rate is not available, poverty among Blacks
in the eleven southern states has probably risen to 39
percent—a rate which now makes almost 2 out of
every 5 Blacks below poverty.[3]

The income of the respondents in this study was almost the exact opposite of the findings concerning the general population of Blacks in southern states. Whereas 39 percent of Blacks in southern states are living in poverty, 33.1 percent of the respondents in this study made $27,000 or more. The income of the Black church laity, in this study, suggests that the Black urban church constituents are economically stable in a time when there is generally a growing increase in the number and rate of Blacks in poverty.

Examination of the Data

Tables two and three contain two of the most important core clusters to this study, "Aggressive Political Leadership" and "Active Concern for the Oppressed."

TABLE 2

AGGRESSIVE POLITICAL LEADERSHIP

1. Participates in an effort to remove an incompetent or ineffective official from school, church, union or government

2. Speaks from the pulpit about political issues

3. Uses principles and methods of social organization for political change

4. Organizes groups to change civil laws which seem in the light of Scripture to be morally wrong

5. Encourages nonunion laborers to organize

6. Is willing to risk arrest to protest social wrongs

7. Works to make sure that all people are free to buy property in areas of their choice

8. Pressures public officials on behalf of the oppressed

TABLE 2 (Continued)

9. Organizes action groups in the congregation to accomplish directly some political or social goal

10. Organizes study groups in congregations or community to discuss public affairs

11. Declares a willingness to run for public office in the community (school board, city council, etc.)

12. Takes an informed position on controversial community issues

---

TABLE 3

ACTIVE CONCERN FOR THE OPPRESSED

---

1. Works toward racial integration in the community

2. Uses authoritative information and facts to meet racism and prejudice in congregation and community

3. Works to integrate people of varying educational, ethnic, and cultural backgrounds into the congregation

4. Acquaints self with the history and aspirations of minority groups and other oppressed people

5. Makes individuals aware of their possible part in causing world poverty

6. Recommends that the parish cut off financial support for institutions (hospitals, missions, etc.) that discriminate against minorities

---

Aggressive Political Leadership is characterized by working actively to protest and change social wrongs. And, Active Concern for the Oppressed is characterized by knowledgeably and earnestly working on behalf of minority and oppressed people.[4]

These two core clusters contain eighteen statements that are more political and/or social than religious. Conversely, there is within the questionnaire items that represent an emphasis upon the religious more than the political. These items have been core clustered to form "Precedence of Evangelistic Goals" (Table 4) which indicates that there is an overwhelming belief that the process of creating a better society is not as important (comparatively) as the evangelization of humanity.[5] There are four items that form this cluster; an explanation of each item is provided near the end of this chapter.

TABLE 4
PRECEDENCE OF EVANGELISTIC GOALS

1. Hold that the church's task of proclaiming the gospel by preaching and teaching over-shadows in importance the task of helping to eliminate physical sufferings of people

2. Frequently approaches strangers to ask about the condition of their soul

3. Priorities in use of time and the belief that the one only way to build an ideal world society is to convert everyone to Christianity

4. Insists that clergy should stick to religion and not concern themselves with social, economic and political questions

The survey contained statements that were rated by the respondents. Each of these statements constituted the dependent variables. The relationship between the independent variables (i.e., denomination, income, education and occupation) and the dependent variables is analyzed using the chi-square statistic. For descriptive purposes, the writer will review and analyze responses to each of the items that constitute the three aforementioned core clusters. Moreover, in the discussion, the writer reduced the original seven category lables to three categories in order to handle the results more concisely and to reduce the possible perception of redundancy.[6] Nevertheless, tables used in this chapter reflect the actual responses.

15

Aggressive Political Leadership

This cluster, "Aggressive Political Leadership," contains twelve statements that describe its content. Each of these statements is discussed relative to the respondents' expectations of the minister. A summary of this cluster is provided following an explication of the last statement.

Participates in an Effort to Remove an
Incompetent or Ineffective Official from
School, Church, Union or Government

According to the data, there was no statistically significant relationship between occupation, education and denomination when these variables were cross-tabulated with responses to the statement, "participates in an effort to remove an incompetent or ineffective official from school, church, union or government." In effect, one's response to this item was not significantly affected by the type of church he/she attended nor one's socio-economic status. This suggests that the respondents were more willing to tolerate the effect of the "Peter Principle" than to forge the issue of eradicating perceived incompetence in officials of school, church, union and government. Moreover, because incompetence or ineffectiveness is the issue, rather than the institution where it occurs, it would be impossible to determine if there would be a difference between one's effort to remove an incompetent in each of the four areas or institution. The "Peter Principle" suggests that individuals tend to rise to their level of incompetence.

> Occupational incompetence is everywhere. . . . We see indecisive politicians posing as resolute statesmen. . . . Limitless are the public servants who are indolent and insolent; military commanders whose behavioral timidity belies their dread-naught rhetoric, and governors whose innate servility prevents their actually governing. In our sophistication, we virtually shrug aside the immoral cleric, corrupt judge, incoherent attorney, author who cannot write and English teachers who cannot spell.[7]

In general, respondents indicated that this item was important; 70.1 percent rated it as important and 19.8 percent said it was undesirable while 10.1 percent had no opinion (see Table 5).

TABLE 5

PERCENTAGE OF RESPONSES TO: PARTICIPATES IN AN EFFORT TO REMOVE AN INCOMPETENT OR INEFFECTIVE OFFICIAL FROM SCHOOL . . .

Responses	Number of Respondents	Percentage
Highly Important	88	26.0
Quite Important	45	13.3
Somewhat Important	74	21.9
Undesirable	22	6.5
Detrimental	75	22.2
Reject Item	20	5.9
Does Not Apply	14	4.1
TOTAL	338	100.0

Speaks From the Pulpit About Political Issues

Basically, three fourths of the respondents indicated that they expected the minister to speak from the pulpit about political issues. An overwhelming 74.6 percent rated this item important and 18.0 percent felt it was undesirable while 7.4 percent had no opinion. Responses to this item suggest that the laity expect the clergy to use the pulpit as a forum for addressing political issues. Table 6 described the responses.

It is important to note that of the total sample of three hundred and thirty-eight respondents, the largest single category of respondents who felt that this item was important consisted of those with some college education. This suggests that there is a pattern of a positive correlation between college education and expectations of the laity relative to the minister's use of the pulpit as a means by

17

which he can address political issues. The relationship is not statistically significant; yet it may have practical significance.

TABLE 6
PERCENTAGE OF RESPONSES TO: SPEAKS FROM THE PULPIT ABOUT POLITICAL ISSUES

Responses	Number of Respondents	Percentage
Highly Important	94	27.8
Quite Important	83	24.5
Somewhat Important	75	22.2
Undesirable	37	10.9
Detrimental	24	7.1
Reject Item	12	3.6
Does Not Apply	13	3.8
TOTAL	338	100.0

Uses Principles and Methods of Social
Organization for Political Change

Two thirds of the respondents to the statement "Uses Principles and Methods of Social Organization for Political Change" indicated that it was important to them and 21.9 percent felt that it was undesirable. This clearly suggests that the majority of persons in the Black church expect the minister to effect political change by the usage of social organization. This strategy demands creativity and imagination in order to be effective in actually bringing about political change. The Black minister's understanding of the principles and methods of social organization will strengthen his ability to usher in political change if he is able to adapt these methods to the particular problem and convince his constituents of the usefulness of this approach. Table 7 describes the frequency of responses to this item.

TABLE 7

**PERCENTAGE OF RESPONSES TO: USES PRINCIPLES
AND METHODS OF SOCIAL ORGANIZATION
FOR POLITICAL CHANGE**

Responses	Number of Respondents	Percentage
Highly Important	63	18.5
Quite Important	96	28.4
Somewhat Important	67	19.8
Undesirable	54	16.0
Detrimental	20	5.9
Reject Item	16	4.7
Does Not Apply	22	6.5
TOTAL	338	100.0

*Organizes Groups to Change Civil Laws Which Seem
in Light of Scripture to be Morally Wrong*

Creating effective methods to change civil laws such as organizing groups is a clear departure from traditional clergy roles. In response to this item, the laity believes that injustice as manifested in civil laws should be confronted by the Black minister. More precisely, an overwhelming 78.6 percent of the respondents felt that it was important to organize groups in order that civil laws which were unjust would be changed to conform with the spirit of the scripture. A meager 5.7 percent felt that this was undesirable, and 6.8 percent had no opinion.

The organization of groups for the explicit purpose of advocating change in civil laws that are perceived to be biblically and morally wrong is conceptually and practically a real part of the Black minister's experience. For example, the Southern Christian Leadership Conference was the result of a minister's ability to organize regional and national support for a change in unjust laws that were first repelled by Rosa Parks. The Montgomery Bus Boycott represented the embryonic stages of a massive movement that reflected the Black minister's ability to organize and mobilize.

TABLE 8

PERCENTAGE OF RESPONSES TO: ORGANIZES GROUPS TO CHANGE CIVIL LAWS WHICH SEEM IN LIGHT OF SCRIPTURE TO BE MORALLY WRONG

Responses	Number of Respondents	Percentage
Highly Important	106	31.4
Quite Important	12	3.6
Somewhat Important	93	27.5
Undesirable	13	3.8
Detrimental	66	19.5
Reject Item	16	4.7
Does Not Apply	32	9.5
TOTAL	338	100.0

Encourages Non-Union Laborers to Organize

Interestingly, less than half of the respondents expected the minister to encourage non-union laborers to organize. Actually 47.3 percent indicated that it was important and 31.7 felt that it was undesirable, while 21 percent had no opinion (see Table 9).

On this particular item, the laity had no definitive expectations of the clergy. Yet, from a historical perspective, urban ministers played a key role in the organized labor strike of the garbagemen of local 1733 of the American Federation of State, County, and Municipal Employees of AFL-CIO in Memphis, Tennessee[8] in the sixties. The respondents to this question may be influenced by the gradual but persistent effort of the business community, with the cooperation of the Reagan administration, to limit the power of unions in effectuating change by influencing policy issues.

TABLE 9
**PERCENTAGE OF RESPONSES TO: ENCOURAGES
NON-UNION LABORERS TO ORGANIZE**

Responses	Number of Respondents	Percentage
Highly Important	38	11.2
Quite Important	51	15.1
Somewhat Important	71	21.0
Undesirable	81	24.0
Detrimental	26	7.7
Reject Item	28	8.3
Does Not Apply	43	12.7
TOTAL	338	100.0

Is Willing to Risk Arrest to Protest Social Wrongs

The majority of the sample, 61.8 percent, indicated that this was an important expectation of the minister while 24.3 percent thought it was undesirable.

The importance of this item reflects the degree to which people who are oppressed would go in order to convince the larger society of the reality of inequity and injustice. Historically, Black ministers have been arrested in the process of protesting segregation and the extensive effect of "Jim Crow" laws. In this connection, explaining why he was in Birmingham in 1966, Martin Luther King, Jr. wrote the following from his jail cell:

> . . . I am in Birmingham because injustice is here . . . Moreover, I am cognizant of the interrelatedness of all communities and states. I cannot sit idly by in Atlanta and not be concerned about what happens in Birmingham. Injustice anywhere is a threat to justice everywhere. We are caught in an inescapable network of mutuality, tied in a single garment of destiny. Whatever affects one directly, affects all indirectly. Never again can we afford to live with the narrow,

provincial 'outside agitator' idea. Anyone who lives
inside the United States can never be considered an
outsider anywhere within its bounds.[9]

It was in this spirit that clergymen Walter Fauntroy, Joseph Lowry and other civil rights advocates were arrested in the fall of 1984 for protesting apartheid in South Africa by staging sit-ins at the South African embassy in Washington, D.C.

Risking arrest to protest social wrongs has been part of the tradition of Black religious leaders, and the laity continue to consider this an important part of the urban minister's responsibility in helping to bring about a just and equitable society (see Table 10 below).

TABLE 10
PERCENTAGE OF RESPONSES TO: IS WILLING TO RISK ARRESTS TO PROTEST SOCIAL WRONGS

Responses	Number of Respondents	Percentage
Highly Important	72	21.3
Quite Important	60	17.8
Somewhat Important	77	22.8
Undesirable	59	17.5
Detrimental	23	6.8
Reject Item	23	6.8
Does Not Apply	24	7.1
TOTAL	338	100.0

Works to Make Sure That All People are Free
To Buy Property in Areas of Their Choice

In responding to this item, 69.2 percent indicated that it was important and 16.8 felt it was not important. Table 11 describes the frequency of responses to this item.

TABLE 11

PERCENTAGE OF RESPONSES TO: WORKS TO MAKE SURE THAT ALL PEOPLE ARE FREE TO BUY PROPERTY IN AREAS OF THEIR CHOICE

Responses	Number of Respondents	Percentage
Highly Important	78	23.1
Quite Important	66	19.5
Somewhat Important	90	26.6
Undesirable	39	11.5
Detrimental	18	5.3
Reject Item	22	6.5
Does Not Apply	25	7.4
TOTAL	338	100.0

The law forbids racial discrimination in housing. Yet racial steering and other methods are sometimes used to assure that persons do not always buy the property they want. Changing the rules and practices rather than the laws, is responsible for the maintenance of unofficial quotas of Blacks in predominantly "white neighborhoods." This same process is used to maintain or foster racial homogeneity in some other neighborhoods.

Moreover, residential housing patterns and their racial composition have an intricate connection to many facets of urban life. There are many auxiliary effects of housing patterns, and the history of neighborhood change reflects the degree to which neighborhoods are homogeneous. Homogeneity can be racial, economic or social, but the degree of homogeneity and diversity within the larger urban environment helps to balance tension in urban communities. Katherine Bradbury et al., state,

> This tension is often partly resolved by two types of spatial separation. One is the separation of residencies from most production activities. . . . The other is the maintenance of separate neighborhoods

23

for different ethnic, social or economic groups—
especially those with significantly different values.[10]

Pressures Public Officials on Behalf of the Oppressed

This is one of the most significant questions in the study because
the existential situation of Blacks and poor in urban areas is one of
oppression in several respects. Oppression manifests itself in
discrimination in employment, inadequate housing, education policy
and in other areas. Moreover, a disproportionate number of those
out of work are Black. The effects of this tragedy are manifested in
depression, suicide and a disbelief in the "so-called" protestant work
ethic.

> Minority young people between the ages of 15 and 26
> years have the highest suicide rate in the country
> according to U.S. National Center for Health Statis-
> tics. Numerous studies have established the connec-
> tion between unemployment and deterioration in
> general health and emotional well being, stress, crime
> and family violence.[11]

TABLE 12

**PERCENTAGE OF RESPONSES TO: PRESSURES PUBLIC
OFFICIALS ON BEHALF OF THE OPPRESSED**

Responses	Number of Respondents	Percentage
Highly Important	89	26.3
Quite Important	63	18.6
Somewhat Important	91	26.9
Undesirable	44	13.0
Detrimental	18	5.3
Reject Item	16	4.7
Does Not Apply	17	5.0
TOTAL	338	100.0

The effects of oppression have immeasurable consequences as
indicated above. In response to the statement, "Pressures public

officials on behalf of the oppressed," 71.9 percent considered it important while 18.3 percent thought it was not important.

Organizes Action Groups in the Congregation
to Accomplish Directly Some Political or Social Goal

A decisive majority of the respondents indicated that this item was important (72.2 percent) while less than twenty percent (19.8) felt it was not important. A minuscule 8 percent had no opinion regarding this item (see Table 13 below).

TABLE 13
PERCENTAGE OF RESPONSES TO: ORGANIZES ACTION GROUPS IN THE CONGREGATION TO ACCOMPLISH DIRECTLY SOME POLITICAL GOAL

Responses	Number of Respondents	Percentage
Highly Important	74	21.9
Quite Important	68	20.1
Somewhat Important	102	30.2
Undesirable	47	13.9
Detrimental	20	5.9
Reject Item	15	4.4
Does Not Apply	12	3.6
TOTAL	338	100.0

Organizes Study Groups in Congregation
or Community to Discuss Public Affairs

In response to the above statement, 69.2 percent of the sample indicated that this statement was important while 18.9 percent felt it was undesirable and 11.8 percent had no opinion (Table 14).

TABLE 14

PERCENTAGE OF RESPONSES TO: ORGANIZES STUDY GROUPS . . . TO DISCUSS PUBLIC AFFAIRS

Responses	Number of Respondents	Percentage
Highly Important	73	21.6
Quite Important	72	21.3
Somewhat Important	89	26.3
Undesirable	49	14.5
Detrimental	15	4.4
Reject Item	18	5.3
Does Not Apply	22	6.5
TOTAL	338	100.0

The organization of study groups in order to discuss public affairs is the beginning of the process of policy analysis. It takes an organized effort to meaningfully impact upon urban policy; therefore, the high percentage of laity who felt that this was important suggests that such practices would have considerable support. Study groups would determine priority items that should be analyzed. This is in effect the beginning of political activity that will inevitably escalate. Yet, there are limitations.

> The factors that limit political activity are of cardinal importance in understanding public affairs. Activity is costly. It eats up time and energy. . . . One must attend meetings, listen to or participate in discussion, write letters, attempt to persuade (or be persuaded by) others, and engage in other such time-consuming labors. This means devoting less time to the job, to the children and to hobbies. Yet these private activities are the primary interest of most people, and so the cost of participation in public affairs seems greater than the return.[12]

The limits and constraints of participating in this process should be a part of the study group's focus in order that the discussion of public affairs will not be a banal exercise in polemics that oftentimes characterize such discussions, but rather a creative and pragmatic experience in understanding the serious effects of public policy upon the oppressed.

The minister who organizes such groups and focuses on the issues that are important to the advancement of an equitable urban environment will meet the expressed need of his/her constituents by facilitating their interests and in effect nurturing community power.

*Declares a Willingness to Run for Public Office
in the Community (School Board, City Council, Etc.)*

Clearly the majority of respondents indicated that this item was important. Yet there was no overwhelming expectation from a comparative perspective. Sixty-three (63.0) percent felt that this item was important while 26.6 percent felt it was not important and 10.3 percent had no opinion.

Inasmuch as a majority of the sample did indicate that this was important, the urban minister who is seeking public office or occupies public office has the support of the laity. More precisely, the majority of persons who attend the Black church expect the minister to be willing to run for political office. However, a willingness to run for office is not the same as actually running for office. Although the laity may expect the minister to declare a willingness to run for office, this does not mean that he will necessarily be supported by all of them. Moreover, the 26.6 percent who felt it was not important may actually be opposed to the minister running for office. If this were the case, the minister would have a very difficult time balancing the support and the opposition. However, the fact remains that a majority of the Black church laity want the minister to seek public office.

TABLE 15

**PERCENTAGE OF RESPONSES TO: DECLARES A
WILLINGNESS TO RUN FOR PUBLIC OFFICE
IN THE COMMUNITY**

Responses	Number of Respondents	Percentage
Highly Important	69	20.4
Quite Important	65	19.2
Somewhat Important	79	23.4
Undesirable	61	18.0
Detrimental	29	8.6
Reject Item	14	4.1
Does Not Apply	21	6.2
TOTAL	338	100.0

*Takes an Informed Position on Controversial
Community Issues*

Seventy-eight and seven-tenths percent of the respondents indicated that they expected the minister to take an informed position on controversial community issues. This suggests that the Black urban laity want to be well represented by clergy who speak on their behalf. Also, it indicates that controversial issues should be studied and approached analytically and from a substantive perspective—not in an impetuous fashion. This is not to indicate that the laity expect an insipid approach but rather an ability to synthesize the cognitive and affective approach in explicating controversial community issues. The rule is to begin somewhere and keep at it. For there are few issues that cannot be mastered."[13]

Furthermore, the data indicated that 11.6 percent of the respondents felt that taking an informed position was not important and 9.7 percent had no opinion (see Table 16).

TABLE 16

PERCENTAGE OF RESPONSES TO: TAKES AN INFORMED POSITION ON CONTROVERSIAL COMMUNITY ISSUES

Responses	Number of Respondents	Percentage
Highly Important	99	29.3
Quite Important	89	26.3
Somewhat Important	78	23.1
Undesirable	28	8.3
Detrimental	11	3.3
Reject Item	15	4.4
Does Not Apply	18	5.3
TOTAL	338	100.0

Summary and Conclusions of Aggressive Political Leadership

Each of the statements that constituted the cluster "Aggressive Political Leadership" was rated important by a majority of the respondents. The items covered a wide range of political activities and the respondents indicated that they expected the Black urban minister to provide aggressive political leadership relative to these problems. This indicates, as we had instinctively felt, that the suffering and oppression of people in urban areas cannot be eradicated by passive and detached acknowledgement of the problem nor by sterile homilies on hunger or recondite discourses on church dogmatics. The Black church laity expect the minister to provide aggressive political leadership in facing the problems of incompetent or ineffective school, church or government officials, organizing groups to change civil laws and lobbying on behalf of the oppressed, etc.

The mean level of importance for all of the statements that constituted this cluster, "Aggressive Political Leadership," was 68.5 percent. This indicates that nearly 7 out of every 10 respondents to these statements rated them important in terms of what they expected of the Black urban minister. This clearly suggests that the constituents of the Black urban church expect the minister not only to provide spiritual leadership, but aggressive political leadership as well.

Active Concern for the Oppressed

This cluster, "Active Concern for the Oppressed," consists of six statements that effectively describe its content. These statements are discussed individually in order to provide a description of the respondents' expectation of the Black Black urban minister.

Works Toward Racial Integration in the Community

In 1977, Alan Pifer, the president of the Carnegie Corporation wrote,

> At least 80 percent of all American families today live
> in segregated neighborhoods, white or Black. De
> facto, the United States is still two nations.[14]

This indicting characterization of America by the (then) president of one of this country's leading philanthropic foundations indicates the magnitude of the chasm between the races that has resulted in a dichotomous system of housing accommodation, education facilities, etc. This clearly suggests that the Black urban minister faces a situation that has not manifested any cataclysmic changes resulting from de jure efforts to dismantle the reality of segregation. In effect the law has created more subtle and ingenious ways to circumvent its mandates relative to most forms of substantive sharing of power and property vis-a-vis integration.

Inasmuch as racial integration is not a fact in spite of all the civil rights, anti-discrimination and fair housing laws, the Black church laity expect the minister to help bring about a more balanced and equitable system. In this connection, an overwhelming 82 percent of the respondents indicated that they expected the minister to work toward racial integration in the community. This reflects virtual unanimity among the Black urban church laity regarding this issue because only 9.8 percent felt it was not important.

TABLE 17
PERCENTAGE OF RESPONSES: WORKS TOWARD RACIAL INTEGRATION IN THE COMMUNITY

Responses	Number of Respondents	Percentage
Highly Important	163	48.2
Quite Important	55	16.3
Somewhat Important	58	17.2
Undesirable	22	6.5
Detrimental	11	3.3
Reject Item	16	4.7
Does Not Apply	13	3.8
TOTAL	338	100.0

The desire for racial integration in the community is clearly expressed by the Black urban laity. This indicates that segregation is not an imagined phenomenon, but real and concrete as evidenced by the facts. Moreover, it suggests that in spite of the law and rhetoric of equality, there is still a need for real integration.

> In fact, real integration is still very much more a hope (or fear) than a reality in most areas of the country because of the almost irresistible impact of residential segregation. We simply do not know, therefore, what the effects of true integration practiced over several generations would be. . . .[15]

Ironically, the chance for thorough integration of public schools is continually decreasing because of those who refuse to accept the equality of all people. Though our society is pluralistic, it continues to treat non-whites with discrimination and inequality. Racial integration continues to be a future goal—not a present reality.

In response to this item, 73.1 percent of the respondents indicated that it was important to discuss racism and prejudice with facts and authoritative information (Table 18). This suggests that the laity are concerned with documented facts rather than conjecture. Because of the emotional and oftentimes irrational approach used in confronting racism and prejudice, it is important to gather the facts in order to effectively address the problem. For an example of facts on institutional racism and prejudice see Appendix G.[16]

TABLE 18
PERCENTAGE OF RESPONSES TO: SPEAKS FROM THE PULPIT ABOUT POLITICAL ISSUES

Responses	Number of Respondents	Percentage
Highly Important	105	31.1
Quite Important	74	21.9
Somewhat Important	68	20.1
Undesirable	35	10.4
Detrimental	20	5.9
Reject Item	19	5.6
Does Not Apply	17	4.0
TOTAL	338	100.0

These tables (Appendix G) represent authoritative information compiled by the U.S. Census Bureau, the Commerce Department and other research organizations. These facts have been collected and published by the Council on Interracial Books for Children under the title, *Fact Sheets on Institutional Racism*. The information contained in the aforesaid tables represent statistical facts on income earned by Whites and Blacks, unemployment rates by race, sex, age and education. Additionally, the types of jobs held by minorities (see Appendix G) suggest that discrimination and racism may be factors that contribute to a minuscule percentate of minorities in managerial positions while a disproportionate percentage occupy positions as laborers and service workers. The use of authoritative information and facts to combat racism and prejudice was very important to the respondents in this study.

Though statistical facts on income, education, unemployment and the types of jobs held by minorities are difficult to challenge, the interpretation of these facts differ considerably. The neoconservatives are less likely to attribute large discrepancies in income and education between Blacks and Whites, to racism and prejudice. Therefore, the victims of these statistics are left explaining why they have failed to succeed in a system that offers "equal opportunity" to all.

Furthermore, Edward Banfield in *The Unheavenly City* and George Gilder in *Wealth and Poverty* suggest that racism and prejudice in today's society is more myth than reality. These writers represent an increasing cadre of scholars who argue that reasons other than racism and prejudice account for Blacks and minorities being disproportionately unemployed and occupying low level jobs. Indeed, they offer an alternative interpretation (to the one heretofore expressed) of the figures in Appendix G.

Additionally, in response to this item, 16.3 percent indicated that it was not important while 10.5 percent had no opinion (see Table 18).

*Works to Integrate People of Varying Educational,
Ethnic and Cultural Background into the Congregation*

One major criticism of the Black church has focused on the fact that it remains a basically segregated institution twenty years after other institutions have become partially integrated or desegregated. It is also argued that the Black minister who was a key actor in effectuating change in other segments of society has failed to coalesce the races in the practice of religion. While it is a fact that Black churches remain basically Black, the reasons cannot necessarily be attributed to the minister's lack of encouragement nor the laity's passivity. Inasmuch as integration has been a painful process in the public sector accomplished only by legal duress, it is too simplistic to suggest that a few reasons are responsible for the present racial status of the Black church. Nevertheless, the data in this study indicate that an overwhelming 82 percent of the respondents felt it was important for the minister to work to integrate the congregation ethnically, culturally and educationally. Again, the laity are suggesting that the Black urban minister work toward creating a heterogeneous congregation, i.e., not just of different races but multiculturally, socially and economically. Less than 10 percent of the respondents felt this item was not important and 8.3 percent had no opinion (Table 19).

TABLE 19
PERCENTAGE OF RESPONSES TO: WORKS TO INTEGRATE PEOPLE OF VARYING EDUCATIONAL, ETHNIC AND CULTURAL BACKGROUND . . .

Responses	Number of Respondents	Percentage
Highly Important	150	44.4
Quite Important	71	21.0
Somewhat Important	56	16.6
Undesirable	16	4.7
Detrimental	17	5.0
Reject Item	10	3.0
Does Not Apply	18	5.3
TOTAL	338	100.0

Acquaints Self With the History and Aspirations
of Minority Groups and Other Oppressed People

In response to this item, 77.8 percent of the respondents indicated that it was important while 13.7 percent felt it was not important.

The importance of this item to the urban laity indicated that they expect the minister to be broad-minded and empathetic. Moreover, the minister is better able to understand and evaluate his own predicament if he is familiar with the history and hopes of others who have had similar political, legal, economic and social experiences. Understanding the forces of oppression that impinge upon other minorities regardless of their nomenclature should create a necessary sensitivity to the condition of others who suffer from kindred forms of inhuman treatment—oppression (see Table 20).

Makes Individuals Aware of Their Possible Part in Causing World Poverty

World poverty is a growing catastrophe. Less Developed Countries of the Third World have not reaped the benefits of the New International Economic Order to the extent that poverty has been eradicated. The United Nations Development Program has been charged with perpetuating self-sufficiency on the part of the LCD's. The definitive yardstick of UNDP's capabilities rests in its ability to diminish world poverty and expand the frontiers of human and economic opportunity throughout the developing world.

The state of poverty and hunger in Ethiopia gained world-wide attention because it was representative of the dehumanizing effects of poverty wherever it is found.

Poverty is not simply a distant reality, but, it exists in the urban centers of the United States.

> In 1970 there were 25.5 million poverty stricken persons in America. An increase of 1.2 million over 1969. . . . Approximately 8.2 million (30 percent) of the nation's poor live in central cities, and 5.2 million (21 percent) live in the metropolitan areas surrounding them.[17]

In response to this item, 75.1 percent of the respondents indicated that it was important for the minister to make people aware of their part in causing world poverty while 16.9 percent indicated that it was not important.

TABLE 20

**PERCENTAGE OF RESPONSES TO: ACQUAINTS SELF
WITH THE HISTORY AND ASPIRATIONS OF
MINORITY GROUPS AND OTHER OPPRESSED PEOPLE**

Responses	Number of Respondents	Percentage
Highly Important	120	35.5
Quite Important	82	10.1
Somewhat Important	61	24.3
Undesirable	34	13.6
Detrimental	12	18.0
Reject Item	16	4.7
Does Not Apply	13	3.8
TOTAL	338	100.0

TABLE 21

**PERCENTAGE OF RESPONSES TO: MAKES
INDIVIDUALS AWARE OF THEIR POSSIBLE PART
IN CAUSING WORLD POVERTY**

Responses	Number of Respondents	Percentage
Highly Important	97	28.7
Quite Important	72	21.3
Somewhat Important	85	25.1
Undesirable	45	13.3
Detrimental	12	3.5
Reject Item	13	3.8
Does Not Apply	14	4.1
TOTAL	338	100.0

Invidious discrimination as well as discrimination based upon sex is illegal and too blatant to be practiced overtly. Moreover, most American institutions believe in the sacrosanctity of the concept of law such that any blatant violation of the law is meticulously avoided. Nevertheless, the results of discrimination are often more obvious than the cause because the results can be documented in quantitative terms.

In response to this item, 52.9 percent of the respondents indicated that they expected the minister to recommend that the church cease providing financial support to institutions that discriminate against minorities. This is not an overwhelming majority because an impressive 25.2 percent indicated that it was undesirable to cut off financial support. This suggests that the Black laity are not overwhelmingly unified on this particular item. This can be attributed to several factors. First, the laity may be reluctant to believe that eleemosynary institutions would discriminate against minorities. Secondly, some may believe that discrimination is nonexistent. Others may view discrimination as a myth. In this connection, George Gilder states,

> One of the problems in dealing with the expanding array of claims of discrimination—reaching far beyond the obvious and paramount victims in American history, the Blacks—is that anyone looking for bias can find it. . . . The last thirty years in America, however, have seen a relentless and thoroughly successful advance against old prejudices to the point that it is now virtually impossible to find in a position of power a serious racist. Gaps in income between truly comparable Blacks and Whites have nearly closed. Problems remain, but it would seem genuinely difficult to sustain the idea that America is still oppressive and discriminatory.[18]

The demythologizing of discrimination can only be achieved by first recognizing its existence. Clearly a majority of the Black church laity expect the minister to respond to discrimination against minorities by withholding economic support.

TABLE 22

PERCENTAGE OF RESPONSES TO: RECOMMENDS THAT THE PARISH CUT OFF FINANCIAL SUPPORT FOR INSTITUTIONS THAT DISCRIMINATE . . .

Responses	Number of Respondents	Percentage
Highly Important	86	25.4
Quite Important	42	12.4
Somewhat Important	51	15.1
Undesirable	57	16.9
Detrimental	28	8.3
Reject Item	34	10.1
Does Not Apply	40	11.8
TOTAL	338	100.0

Summary and Conclusions to Active Concern for the Oppressed

The statements that constituted this cluster demanded that the minister be involved in the actual dismantling of the mechanisms that sustain racism, prejudice, segregation and discrimination. The oppressed are the victims of these mechanisms that have been embodied in the structure of society. "Active Concern for the Oppressed" is characterized by working toward racial integration, using authoritative facts to combat racism and prejudice, acquainting oneself with the history and aspirations of minorities, etc. The majority of the respondents indicated that the items in the cluster were important relative to their expectations of the minister.

The mean level of importance for all the statements that constituted this cluster, "Active Concern for the Oppressed," was 78 percent. This indicates that approximately 8 out of every 10 respondents to the statements comprising this cluster felt that it was important for the Black urban minister to be actively concerned for the oppressed. This suggests that the Black urban church laity expect the minister to be more than a traditional spiritual leader. They expect him to contribute to bringing about a just and equitable society by helping those who are oppressed.

Precedence of Evangelistic Goals

This core cluster, "Precedence of Evangelistic Goals" contains four statements that describe its content. Each of these statements is explained relative to the respondents' expectations of the Black urban minister. Moreover, statements in this cluster provide a traditional description of expectations of the minister.

Holds that the Church's Task of Proclaiming the Gospel
by Preaching and Teaching Overshadows in Importance the Task
of Helping to Eliminate Physical Sufferings of People

This item reflects the traditional role and expectation of the minister, i.e., proclamation of the gospel. In response to this item 62.1 percent indicated that it was important while 25.2 percent felt it was not important.

This item creates a dichotomy between preaching and teaching and helping to eliminate the physical suffering of people. In actuality, there is a nexus between the two. "I have come to set at liberty those who are oppressed."[19] This statement is the archetype of liberation theology from a christological perspective.

The chi-square statistic indicated that the difference in assessment by denomination was statistically significant (P = .0056). Table 33 in Appendix E contains complete information on this relationship. The findings also indicated that the difference in education, congregation size and income was not statistically significant.

Responses to this item suggest that the Black laity continues to respect and hold in high esteem the preaching of the gospel. Preaching and teaching are very important in the life of the church. Moreover, the spiritual power inherent in preaching and teaching helps the believer to deal with the eradication of physical suffering. The healing power of the gospel is real to the believer.

TABLE 23

**PERCENTAGE OF RESPONSES TO: HOLDS THAT
THE CHURCH'S TASK OF PROCLAIMING THE GOSPEL
BY PREACHING AND TEACHING OVERSHADOW . . .
HELPING TO ELIMINATE SUFFERING**

Responses	Number of Respondents	Percentage
Highly Important	98	29.0
Quite Important	44	13.0
Somewhat Important	68	20.1
Undesirable	51	15.1
Detrimental	34	10.1
Reject Item	16	4.7
Does Not Apply	27	8.0
TOTAL	338	100.0

*Frequently Approaches Strangers to Ask
About the Condition of Their Souls*

This item represents an often practiced method of evangelism, albeit simplistic. Questions regarding the soul of man have occupied the great religious philosophers, i.e., Aristotle, Eckhart, Kant, Plato and Plotinus.[20] Nevertheless, the condition of one's soul is a concern in the practice of religious evangelism.

This method of evangelism leaves a lot to be desired, but it continues to be a popular practice in the church. People want to feel that the church has not become an isolated institution, practicing its rituals and worship only among its own members. There are strangers within the church and in the community who need to be approached, consoled and helped. Although there is a growing risk in such approaching strangers, it remains a viable method of contributing to church growth and practicing the faith.

TABLE 24

**PERCENTAGE OF RESPONSES TO: FREQUENTLY
APPROACHES STRANGERS TO ASK ABOUT THE
CONDITION OF THEIR SOULS**

Responses	Number of Respondents	Percentage
Highly Important	73	21.6
Quite Important	50	14.8
Somewhat Important	82	24.3
Undesirable	69	20.4
Detrimental	28	8.3
Reject Item	10	3.0
Does Not Apply	26	7.7
TOTAL	338	100.0

In response to this item, 60.7 percent of the respondents indicated that it was important and 28.7 percent felt it was not important. An additional 10.7 percent had no opionion (see Table 24 below).

*Priorities in Use of Time Indicate the Belief that
the One and Only Way to Build and Ideal World
Society is to Convert Everyone to Christianity*

In response to this item, 72.5 percent of persons responding to the survey indicated that this item was important. Like wise, 16.9 percent indicated it was not important and 10.6 had no opinion (see Table 25).

This item clearly reflects a belief in the evangelization of humanity; and an overwhelming percentage of the respondents expect the minister to prioritize his time accordingly. Responses to this particular item also indicated that the laity expect the Black urban minister to be a religious and political leader.

41

TABLE 25

**PERCENTAGE OF RESPONSES TO: THE WAY TO BUILD
AN IDEAL WORLD SOCIETY IS TO CONVERT
EVERYONE TO CHRISTIANITY**

Responses	Number of Respondents	Percentage
Highly Important	99	29.3
Quite Important	74	21.9
Somewhat Important	72	21.3
Undesirable	31	9.2
Detrimental	26	7.7
Reject Item	18	5.3
Does Not Apply	18	5.3
TOTAL	338	100.0

*Insists that Clergy Should Stick to Religion
and not Concern Themselves with Social,
Economic and Political Questions*

If there is a prototypal statement in this cluster to characterize a preference of concern for evangelistic goals, it is represented by the aforesaid statement. In response to this item, 46.7 percent of the sample indicated that this item was important. This suggests that less than half of the laity felt that the minister should stick to religion and not be concerned with social, economic and political questions (see Table 26).

This percentage represents the lowest of any "important" responses in all categories or clusters. Moreover, this suggests that the Black urban clergy are expected to be concerned with the existential situation such that he/she does not lose focus of the environment. Moreover, this finding suggests that there must be a balance between the traditionally religious and eschatological focus of the church vis-a-vis the social and political focus. In this connection, 36.7 percent of the respondents indicated that it was not important for the minister to stick only to religion and 16.6 percent had no opinion.

TABLE 26

PERCENTAGE OF RESPONSES TO: INSISTS THAT CLERGY SHOULD STICK TO RELIGION AND NOT BE CONCERNED WITH . . . POLITICAL QUESTIONS

Responses	Number of Respondents	Percentage
Highly Important	60	17.8
Quite Important	42	12.4
Somewhat Important	56	16.6
Undesirable	79	23.4
Detrimental	45	13.3
Reject Item	29	8.6
Does Not Apply	27	8.0
TOTAL	338	100.0

The chi-square statistic indicated that the difference in denomination, income, education and congregation size was not significant.

Summary and Conclusions to Precedence of Evangelistic Goals

Unlike the other two clusters, this cluster of statements was used because it represented the opposite emphasis. "Precedence of Evangelistic Goals" represents the traditional understanding of ministry with emphasis on proclaiming the gospel by preaching and teaching, asking strangers about the condition of their souls, proselytizing and insisting that clergy should stick to religion. These evangelistic or relatively traditional religious statements present a clear contrast to the statements found in the other two previously mentioned clusters.

The mean level of importance for all of the statements that constituted this cluster, "Precedence of Evangelistic Goals," was 60.25 percent. This was the lowest of the three clusters which indicates that fewer respondents felt that the evangelization of society was as important as providing strong political leadership and expressing concern for the oppressed. Nevertheless, the fact that 60.25 percent of the respondents indicated that they expect the minister to focus on evangelistic goals, does suggest that there is not an absolute dichotomy in the laity's expectations of the clergy. There is a "both/and" phenomenon at work here which seems to indicate that the Black church laity expect the minister to be "priest" as well as social and political leader.

Overall Summary of the Core Cluster Responses

The aggregate data indicated that the mean levels of importance for each of the core clusters were 68.5, 78.0 and 60.25 percent respectively. This suggests that there is no true dichotomy in laity expectations of clergy relative to the religious and the socio-political. Yet, the category "Active Concern for the Oppressed" has the highest combined percentage of important responses (see Figure 1).

Fig. 1. Mean Level of Importance by Cluster

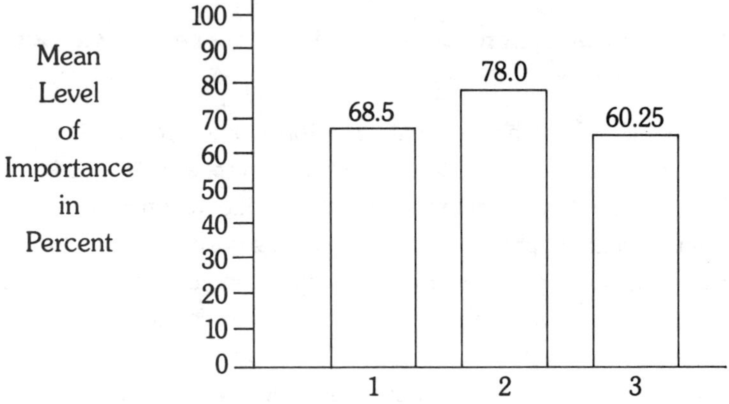

[1]Aggressive Political Leadership
[2]Active Concern for the Oppressed
[3]Precedence of Evangelistic Goals

The statements in each of the clusters seem to be important to a large percentage of the respondents. This suggests a nexus between the socio-political and the religious that may be unique to the Black urban church laity because of their experience in the church and society.

Results of the Hypothesis

Laity in Different Denominations Have Different
Expectations of the Minister's Active Involvement
in Social and Political Ministries in Urban Areas

There was not an overwhelming statistically significant relationship between the independent variable, denomination, and a majority of the dependent variables in the survey. Nevertheless, the chi-square statistic indicated that the difference in denomination was statistically significant regarding each of the following three variables.

1. Organizes groups to change civil laws which seem in light of scripture to be morally wrong.
2. Works to integrate people of varying educational, ethnic, and cultural backgrounds into the congregation.
3. Holds that the church's task of proclaiming the gospel by preaching and teaching overshadows in importance the task of helping to eliminate physical sufferings of people.

A specific in-depth analysis of the data indicate that a majority of the respondents under different denominations rated the aforesaid items "important." Whereas there is a statistical significance, an analysis does not support the existence of a substantive significance. Therefore, there seems to be no practical significance to the statistical difference because a large majority of each congregation rated the aforesaid items "important" (see Appendix E, Tables 27, 28, and 29).

Each of the aforesaid variables relates to ecclesiology in some way, however small. More precisely, each of the variables seem to be less oriented toward discerning social and political involvement than many of the others. Moreover, there was no statistically significant difference between denomination and the majority of the dependent variables. Taken as a whole, the null hypothesis is true. When viewed individually there is a statistically significant difference between denomination and the three dependent variables heretofore discussed.

Laity with High Socio-Economic Status (as Measured)
by Income and Education) have Higher Expectations
in Terms of Social and Political Involvement
than Laity of Low Socio-Economic Status

There was a statistically significant difference, according to the chi-square statistic, regarding the education and income (see Appendix E, Tables 30 and 31) of the respondent and his/her response to the following item:

1. Priorities in use of time indicate the belief that the one and only way to build an ideal world society is to convert everyone to Christianity.

This was the only dependent variable when cross-tabulated with education that had a statistically significant chi-square. Moreover, the aforesaid statement addresses the traditional perception of the minister and confirms the fact that there remains a dichotomy in the laity's expectations of the minister. While the majority of the persons who attend the Black urban church expect the minister to be involved in social and political activities, they also expect him to use his time to proselytize others to the Christian religion. This is not a contradiction because it should be understood that the church is still basically a religious institution. Moreover, there is an interrelationship between the religious and the political in the Black community as has been discussed in Chapter One.

Secondly, the chi-square statistic indicated that there was a statistically significant difference (P = .0467) in the respondent's income and his/her response to "Priorities in use of time indicate the belief that the one and only way to build an ideal world society is to convert everyone to Christianity." Moreover, the chi-square statistic indicated that there was a significant difference (P = .0230) and (P = .0410) in the respondent's occupation (see Tables 32 and 33) and his or her response to the following items.

1. Works to integrate people of varying educational, ethnic, and cultural backgrounds of the congregation.
2. Acquaints self with the history and aspirations of minority groups and other oppressed people.

Summary of the Findings

The majority of the statements that constituted each of the three core clusters—Aggressive Political Leadership, Active Concern for the Oppressed and Precedence of Evangelistic Goals—were rated important by the respondents. Of the three core clusters, "Active Concern for the Oppressed" received the highest percentage of "important" responses from the laity. An impressive 78 percent of the respondents to the statements in this cluster felt that they were important in terms of their expectations of the minister. This cluster was followed by "Aggressive Political Leadership" with a mean level of importance of 68.5 percent and "Precedence of Evangelistic Goals" with a mean level of importance of 60.25 percent.

The findings suggest that the Black church laity expect the minister to be a spiritual leader as well as a social and political leader.

A macrocosmic analysis of the results suggests that neither socio-economic status nor denominational affiliation was statistically significant factors in the responses to the questionnaire. From a microcosmic perspective, the respondents' denomination made a statistically significant difference in the following three variables.

1. Organizes groups to change civil laws which seem in light of scripture to be morally wrong.
2. Works to integrate people of varying educational, ethnic, and cultural backgrounds into the congregtion.
3. Holds that the church's task of proclaiming the gospel by preaching and teaching overshadows in importance the task of helping to eliminate physical sufferings of people.

Because denominational differences affected responses to only three dependent variables and, because these variables were in three different core clusters, the writer accepts the null hypothesis that: there is no relationship between denominational affiliation and Black laity expectations regarding the urban ministers' social and political involvement.

Socio-economic status, as measured by education and income, is statistically related in the respondents' answers to the following statements:

1. Works to integrate people of varying educational, ethnic, and cultural backgrounds into the congregation.
2. Acquaints self with the history and aspirations of minority groups and other oppressed people.

Again, because socio-economic status was statistically significant for such a minuscule number of variables, we are compelled to conclude that there was no difference between the social and political expectations of laity with high socio-economic status and those with low socio-economic status.

FOOTNOTES

[1] Council on Interracial Books for Children, *Fact Sheets on Institutional Racism* (New York: New York) November 1984, p 27.

[2] *Ibid..*

[3] Steve Suitts, *Patterns of Poverty: A Special Report of the Southern Regional Council* (Atlanta: Southern Regional Council, 1984), p. 7.

[4] Cf. *Ministry In America*, David Schuller, Merton Strommen, Milo Brekke, editors. Specifically in Chapter 5, the sixty-four core clusters and their profiles are given. The present writer draws extensively from these data and uses the same clusters in an effort to contrast the political and the religious. Also, descriptions of the core clusters are extracted from the aforesaid book. Moreover, because these authors have already done the statistical tests that resulted in the core clusters, the present writer did not have to repeat that process.

[5] *Ibid.*, p. 104f.

[6] The original survey asked respondents to rate the items using the following seven item scale: Highly Important, Quite Important, Somewhat Important, Undesirable, Detrimental, Reject Item and Does Not Apply. For purposes of explanation, the writer has combined the seven categories to form three new categories "important," "undesirable" and "no opionion."

[7] Lawrence J. Peter and Raymond Hull, *The Peter Principle* (New York: William Morrow and Company, Inc., 1969), pp. 2, 4.

[8] Richard J. Stillman, II, *Public Administration: Concepts and Cases* (Boston: Houghton Mifflin Company, 1980), p. 112.

[9] Martin Luther King, Jr., *Why We Can't Wait* (New York: Harper and Row, 1964), pp. 78-79.

[10] Katherine Bradbury, et al, *Urban Decline and The Future of American Cities* (Washington: The Brookings Institution, 1982), p. 22.

[11] Jill Nelson, *Black Enterprise*, "Out of Work: The People Behind the Statistics," May 1982, p. 64.

[12] Aaron Wildavsky, *Speak the Truth to Power: The Art and Craft of Policy Analysis* (Boston: Little, Brown and Company, 1979), p. 254.

[13] *Ibid.*, p. 258.

[14] Alan Pifer, *Black Progress: Achievement, Failure and an Uncertain Future* (New York: Carnegie Corporations, 1977), p. 9.

[15] *Ibid.*, p. 11.

[16] Council on Interracial Books for Children, *Fact Sheets on Institutional Racism*, pp. 5-7.

[17] George Henderson, *To Live In Freedom, Human Relations Today and Tomorrow* (Oklahoma: University of Oklahoma Press, 1972), p. 164.

[18] George Gilder, *Wealth and Poverty* (New York: Basic Books, Inc., 1981), p. 128.

[19] Luke 4:18.

[20] For an explanation of the soul, cf. George F. Thomas, *Religious Philosophies of the West* (New York: Charles Scribner's Sons, 1965).

Chapter Three

Ambivalence Among Minister and Laity

The Black urban minister and laity are a part of the church and the world. Their existential reality is conducive to creating feelings of polarity and tension. Inasmuch as evangelistic goals characterize the "priestly" role of the minister and the "activist" role is characterized by active concern for the oppressed and aggressive political leadership, clergy and laity are caught between these two relatively contrary phenomena. Evangelism and politicism, though not mutually exclusive, generally have different goals. However, the condition of Black life in urban America does not allow the minister nor laity the luxury of dichotomizing these concepts. The fact is that the use of evangelism as an instrumentality for socio-economic improvement in the city fails to achieve this accomplishment. Inadequate housing, unemployment, discrimination, and other social and economic atrocities, continue to pervade urban Black America. These conditions contribute to the ambivalence of the minister and laity because the Black church and the larger urban community must co-exist. This coexistence of institutions with contrary feelings, goals and interests is conducive to producing ambivalent attitudes and subsequent behavior. The majority of persons in the Black urban church expect the minister to be socially and politically active by providing aggressive political leadership and active concern for the oppressed; however, the same group wants evangelistic goals to have precedence in the minister's life. This paradox and the inability of the laity to establish a preference regarding their expectations of the minister suggests a level of unsurety that is puzzling. The lack of unanimity inherent in the laity's expectations may be more accurately described as "ambivalence."

Because of the Black church's historical relationship with the white church, Gayraud Wilmore says, "black religion has always been something more and something less than traditional European religion."[1] Nevertheless, the nexus between Black and White religion, however different, continues to exist. The contact between Black slaves and their White masters was bound to leave an indelible imprint upon the minds of both groups. Historically, Blacks have been ambivalent about the relationship—vacillating between levels of caring and not caring, trust and distrust. Additionally, the formal worship of Blacks was often held in the presence of Whites within their church building or with Blacks as congregants and a White man as minister. The religious situation was the epitome of paradox because the white preacher represented the oppressor vis-a-vis the bearer of a message of the gospel. He was both prophet and propagator of the status quo. This dualism, represented by word and deed, clearly characterized the master/slave relationship. Moreover, because Black religion is a combination of African and European traditions, the Black laity represent an amalgamation of the elements that constitute both heritages. This makes the Black laity and clergy unique such that they harbor vestiges of both cultures which manifest themselves in a tension that suggests the presence of inherent ambivalence.

This chapter will examine several theories or reasons for the ambivalent attitudes of the laity relative to their expectations of the minister. The basic reasons expounded upon will be selfishness, narcissism, fear of discrimination in employment and the fear of physical harm or death.

Selfishness: An Inherent Element in the Laity's Ambivalence

Black church laity are very concerned about the minister's social and political involvement in the community because his involvement helps to legitimize the interests, frustrations and complaints voiced by those who are essentially powerless in effectuating positive change. However, the Black church laity are also reluctant to fully endorse the minister's involvement because they believe that his participation in "outside" activities will mean that he will have less time to pursue evangelistic goals. Inasmuch as evangelism, in its many forms, still represents the prototype of traditional ministry, social and political efforts, however progressive and humanitarian, appear to be viewed with a degree of skepticism. The skeptics are not without understanding; indeed they fully understand the needs of the community and the necessity for the minister to become involved in the social and political process that will help to address the urban situation of distress and despair. However, the laity are also motivated by a natural selfishness that is mostly innocent. They simply want "their" minister for themselves and some pastors tend to accept that "selfishness" as an expression of love and overwhelming interest in his well being. However, genuine Christian love is selfless and understanding, i.e., always focusing upon the needs of others.

> Love is patient, love is kind, and is not jealous; love does not brag and is not arrogant, does not act unbecomingly; it does not seek its own, is not provoked, does not take into account a wrong suffered . . .[2]

The minister must be adept enough to balance the needs of the laity with the needs of the larger community. Additionally, the laity do not exist in isolation and the church is not immune from the problems that plague urban America. In reality, the laity constitute both the church and the community. This existential reality creates some tension and ambivalence regarding the minister's active involvement in the community because Black pastors, educators and political leaders have failed to develop the proper linkages between the church and city hall. The fact that the Black church laity feel ambivalent or unsure about their expectations of the minister—i.e., whether he should be either "priest" or "politician" suggests that more teaching has to be done by the pastors in order to justify and explain the need for the Black church laity to recognize the interrelationship between the church and the urban community. The ambivalence is based on a type of subliminal desire to keep the church out of the political sphere of society. However, some of the greatest white proponents of the separation of church and state are probably in church on Sunday and are in the State Department and other areas of government on Monday. The views of their churches become an extension of the corporation or government philosophy and vice versa. The Black laity should understand that they are potentially the most powerful reservoir of political strength in urban America. If organized, taught and encouraged properly, this group of people could literally effectuate a cataclysmic change in the nature of the urban milieu.

The parochial view of the minister embraced by the Black church laity will have to be overcome. Indeed too many laypersons perceive the world in a narrow and confining way. This means that the community is perceived and discussed in limited geographic and political terms. Instead of viewing the entire city as "the community" the laity have parochialized the city and helped to establish a limited view of "neighborhoods." Black laity must not allow spatial distances—geographical or social, to circumvent the belief that unity and not fragmentation will effectuate meaningful social, political and economic change. Where Blacks live within the city, especially if it is in a middle class community, must not cause them to lose focus of the residential status of most of their brothers and sisters. It is understood that where one lives is a measure of social status such that differences in people, at least socially, are readily presumed. However, residential segregation tends to make these differences more easily discernible.

> An address is far more than a convenient way of organizing the supply of public services or of locating an individual in physical space. It also locates him in social space. The address of a person immediately identifies him as a member of a particular social group. . . . So pervasive is this effect that residential location has frequently been used as one of the measures in an individuals' position in local prestige hierarchy.[3]

Narcissism, Anxiety and Ambivalence

Since the social and political emphasis on justice and equality for all during the nineteen sixties, there has been a growing interest in personal achievement and the attainment of individual goals. The spirit of acquisition and self satisfaction has engulfed the church and society such that the laity are stridently pursuing that which is personal and economic, i.e., education, houses, cars, etc. Christopher Lasch in the preface to *The Culture of Narcissism* states that:

> After the political turmoil of the sixties, Americans have retreated to purely personal preoccupations. Having no hope of improving their lives in any of the ways that matter, people have convinced themselves that what matters is psychic self-improvement, getting in touch with their feelings, eating healthy food, taking lessons in ballet or belly-dancing, immersing themselves in the wisdom of the East, jogging, learning how to "relate," overcoming the 'fear of pleasure.' Harmless in themselves, these pursuits, elevated to a program and unwrapped in the rhetoric of authenticity and awareness, signify a retreat from politics and a repudiation of the recent past.[4]

This concentrated effort upon the "self" has also created an anxiety that manifests itself in an inability to clearly discern what the church expects of the minister. "The new narcissist is haunted not by guilt but by anxiety."[5] The anxiety is a product of man's inherent dichotomy. In this connection, Reinhold Niebuhr argues that anxiety is a part of the nature of man. He quotes Soren Kierkegaard by stating,

> Anxiety is the inevitable concomitant of the paradox of freedom and finiteness in which man is involved. Anxiety is the internal precondition of sin. It is the inevitable spiritual state of man, standing in the paradoxical situation of freedom and finiteness.[6]

St. Augustine, John Calvin and Martin Luther were proponents of the view that sin was essentially pride—a view consistent with Pauline theology. Additionally Paul felt that anxiety, tension or ambivalence manifested itself within him as a war between good and evil. This is akin to the tension, or anxiety that manifests itself in the laity. If anxiety is the permanent or inevitable concomitant of freedom and the laity are free to participate in the social, political and economic sphere of society, then that freedom to participate is also the source of their bondage to indecision. This "bondage" manifests itself in the laity's inability to express absolute certainty about their expectations; however, they are as certain as their freedom will allow them to be. Because of their freedom, their positions of comfort, their job security and the general feeling of success, the laity are reluctant to jeopardize this by tampering with controversial social and political issues. More importantly, they love themselves more than they love others. This narcissistic view is partly responsible for the ambivalence that the laity feel about the minister. Niebuhr says that ". . . all human life is involved in the sin of seeking security at the expense of other life."[7] Security for oneself is natural and expected. However, the level of security and the maintenance thereof may affect the laity's inability to decisively and overwhelmingly indicate what they expect the Black Urban Minister to do regarding social and political issues. This becomes more important because the minister's increased social and political involvement may eventually demand the active involvement of the laity. This auxiliary affect of the minister's active involvement may force the laity to proceed cautiously and indecisively because of their dependence on other institutions, i.e., business, government or industry, for a livelihood. Theoretically, they must want to be involved; however, their ambivalence is the product of their self interest rather than their interest in the larger community. This existential dilemma has ontological significance simply because it takes courage to be able to do at least that which we expect of others. This is an element that the laity has not come to grips with in terms of understanding the relationship between expectations of the minister and their participation with equal vigor and commitment. This type of committed participation requires courage. "Courage is self affirmation 'in spite of', that which tends to prevent the self from affirming itself."[8] However, ambivalence is a cross between courage and fear. According to Paul Tillich "fear . . . has a definite object, which can be faced, analyzed, attacked, endured."[9] Consequently, the Black laity are ambivalent about the social and political expectations of the minister because they fear that somehow his activism may be traced back to their encouragement and support. This will make them quasi-activists and may be viewed negatively by their employers and clients. This caution and fear is the essence of narcissism such that it is a tool for survival in a politically conservative society. Additionally, the laity may feel very uneasy about being identified with anyone who has confronted and waged an overt effort to eradicate some of the inequities that their companies or employers have perpetuated.

Racial Discrimination in Employment as a Source of Ambivalence

When one is engaged in active social and political involvement vis-a-vis serving as an urban pastor, he will undoubtedly encounter and experience first hand ambivalence. There exists an intricate connection between what individuals are willing to say and do publicly and the perceived impact of their stance on the ability to keep their job and gain promotions, etc. This is crucial because one's employment status or lack of it has ontological and psychological significance, i.e., one's employment status determines the extent to which one becomes involved in a controversial social or political issue.

The economic stability of the Black church laity is evident by their relatively high median income and educational level. This is in contrast to the increasing numbers of persons throughout the south and the nation who are victims of poverty. However, it is this difference that may account for much of the ambivalence. Persons who are poor, jobless and clearly oppressed are less likely to be ambivalent about their expectations of ministers or their personal involvement because they simply have little or nothing to lose. Conversely the largest percentage of persons used in this work were clearly Black urban professionals (BUPPIES) who earned $27,000 or more. Their ambivalence is connected to their economic survivability which is a direct result of their dependent employment status. These individuals understand the subtleties and the magnitude of discrimination in employment. Additionally they understand that the victims of discrimination are usually Black; therefore, understanding the reality and fear of racial discrimination in employment is one of the reasons for the ambivalence of the laity.

The problem of unemployment and its auxiliary effects are by-products of discrimination. Furthermore, if pressed to its logical conclusion, the nexus between discrimination in employment and the reality of unemployment is so intricately interdependent that the alpha point is impossible to determine. The fact is that a disproportionate number of those out of work is Black. The effects of this tragedy are manifested in depression, suicide, and a rejection of the belief that we live in a "color-blind" society. The full effects of the lack of employment have not been completely determined. However, we suspect that joblessness caused by some form of discrimination accounts for a large percentage of those Blacks who are unsuccessful in finding work.

Covert mechanisms of discrimination are responsible for the over-representative number of Blacks that are unemployed. Every "reputable" company today is committed to equal opportunity and affirmative action. Yet, the people behind the unemployment statistics are disproportionately Black. The new means of discrimination are more subtle and covert than the blatant acts of invidious discrimination that were practiced in the past.[10]

Discrimination in employment is as real as the existence of minorities. It cannot be adequately remedied unless it is first recognized as a reality. Invidious discrimination is hailed as a "thing of the past"; however, the facts indicate that persons who are not white are underpaid, underemployed, disproportionately unemployed, subject to racial slurs when employed, etc.

Discrimination can be based on a potpourri of characteristics, e.g., sex, age, religion, handicaps, etc. The fear of discrimination based on active social and political involvement is also a factor in the ambivalence of the clergy and laity. Discrimination in employment is a phenomenon that must be reckoned with during these times of economic austerity and new federalism. The new tide of conservatism which is evidently committed to totally dismantling any vestiges of the Great Society programs has a profound impact upon employment. Blacks and others can barely survive the practices of discrimination in employment under ordinary circumstances. The latitude given employers in the past must be rejected and consciously opposed by those who are suspect of the system. Additionally, the general social milieu that exists throughout the country today does not look promising for Blacks and minorities in any area.

> Economic recession, expanding unemployment and underemployment, tax and expenditure limitations and a public opinion back lash against affirmative action cloud the future of minorities in urban management.[11]

As of June 1982, there were 42 Black city managers out of a total of 3,000. Surely the future looks bleak, for Blacks and minorities in top management positions in the public sector. The scarcity of minorities in upper level positions will increase, according to some, because the conservative city councils are unwilling to risk employing minorities because of a perceived political liability. Henderson writes,

> The penetration of the city management profession by blacks continues to be difficult. Joining traditional political and administrative resistance to affirmative action programs . . . are the politics of increasingly conservative city councils and the economics of increasingly tight budgets. Some city councils consider even the best qualified black management prospects a political liability and a management risk. This is particularly true in cities with less than 50 percent black population.[12]

Discrimination in employment continues to be a reality too pervasive to ignore and too endemic and malignant to obliterate in a short period of time. There is still hope that the poor will be fed and those who have succumbed to the sickness of despair will find the strength to have hope. Racial discrimination is a vicious monster that is genocidal and, those who are sensitive to the reality of oppression (on any level) because of their existential situation must not only be aware of the existence of racial discrimination in employment, but Blacks must resolve to seriously address the causes of this reality.

The fear of this reality felt and understood by minorities,

continues to plague those who are compelled to fight for social and economic equity by political activism. These persons are ambivalent because they understand the subtleties of the employment market, the necessity to provide for one's family and the need for fairness and equality for all people. The process of deciding to become involved in something that may cause one to suffer discrimination in employment creates ambivalence.

The Fear of Physical Harm and Death as a Source of Ambivalence

The Black urban minister is the leader and symbol of authority and confidence in the church. His responsibility is varied and comprehensive—ranging from performing perfunctory activities such as marriages and baby dedications to preaching, teaching and participating in the eradication of social ills. The minister is a true "father figure" in the church, a role model for many persons who are victims of poverty, discrimination and a host of social and economic problems. The black laity love the minister; however, their love and care help to facilitate the fear of losing him to the whimsical and aberrant behavior of those who wish to physically perpetrate harm upon him. Laity ambivalence (and clergy ambivalence) is due to the fear of losing the minister's leadership skills to some other church or organization or more importantly, permanently losing him because he may be harmed or killed. This "separation anxiety" is similar to the way a child feels when his/her parents leave or plan to leave him alone for an extended period of time. The child is afraid that the parent will not return and feels a sense of abandonment. This is not to suggest that the laity are like children, but rather to indicate that emotional and spiritual attachment to the minister often runs deep.

History has proven that this fear of physical harm and death is justified when a minister is trying to change the status quo by becoming socially and politically active as an advocate of justice and fairness. Nat Turner met his demise because of his efforts to destroy the source of oppression and slavery in Southampton County, Virginia. As a minister his actions were certainly not evangelistic;

instead they were the embodiment of social radicalism. More recent history indicates that Black ministers and laity who have led the effort for social reform, however non-violent their methods, have encountered the violent wrath of the oppressor. Martin Luther King, Jr. was killed because of his social activism. His efforts to bring about a color blind society with "liberty and justice for all" were despised by many and viewed with suspicion by others. Medgar Evers, Emmet Till, Malcolm X, and a host of other Black activists who cannot be accounted for met their deaths through mysterious disappearances or blatant murder. These facts are not easily forgotten. The laity and clergy remember these violent incidents through personal experience or historical documentation. Many Black Americans vividly remember the evening of Dr. King's death, because he was the paradigm of struggle, hope, determination and commitment to righting the social and economic ills of a society that was in complicity with sin and injustice. Dr. King's effort to correct these pathological social problems was contrary to the view of the establishment. This made him a target for those who advocated and perpetrated injustice. The Black clergy and laity continue to live with this painful history recognizing that social and political activism may bring physical harm to the minister and his family.

The historical reality of lynchings, accidental deaths and malicious murder of ministers and other social activists cause some laity to experience serious ambivalence about their minister's interest in political office or participation in other processes of social change. The laity understand that if their leader is killed, their loss is not only emotional and psychological but it is also strategic. They realize that the development of committed clergy takes a long time and when one is taken from this world by the hands of crime, it is not easy to overcome this very real loss. Those who remain are fearful that the next person who occupies the position of leader is equally subject to be violated. The pain and loss are real such that the laity do not want to experience this excruciating pain as a necessary by-product of active social and political involvement. This fear of physical harm is one reason why so many of the laity and clergy are burdened with feelings of ambivalence.

The ambivalence of the Black clergy and laity has its roots in the history of Blacks in America. The reality of slavery as a substantial part of the Black man's past cannot be dismissed as a past inequity that has ceased to impact the present. In the language of W.E.B. DuBois, Blacks possess a "double consciousness" because of the double standard that they have experienced throughout history. He describes it by saying

> After the Egyptian and Indian, the Greek and Roman, the Teuton and Mongolian, the Negro is a sort of seventh son, born with a veil, and gifted with second-sight in this American World, a world which yields him no true self-consciousness but only let's him see himself through the revelation of the other world. It is a peculiar sensation, this double consciousness, this sense of always looking at one's self through the eyes of others, of measuring one's soul by the tape of a world that looks on in amused contempt and pity. One even feels his twoness—an American, a Negro; two souls, two thoughts, two unreconciled strivings; two warring ideals in one dark body, whose dogged strength alone keeps it from being torn asunder.[13]

The aforesaid words originally from *The Souls of Black Folks*, clearly describe the nature of the present Black clergy and laity in urban America. This ambivalence is a pathological phenomenon that has followed the Black American from the slave era of the sixteenth and seventeenth centuries to the present time.

FOOTNOTES

[1] Gayraud Wilmore's *Black Religion and Black Radicalism* explains the African and American connections that influenced the reality of Black religious practices in America. The melding of the two traditions has contributed to the uniqueness of the Black Church experience. For a more detailed analysis read the first three chapters.

[2] Bible, New American Standard, 1 Corinthians:14:5-6.

[3] Ducan Timms, *The Urban Mosaic: Towards a Theory of Residential Differentiation* (Cambridge: The University Press, 1971), p. 211.

[4] Christopher Lasch, *The Culture of Narcissism: American Life in An Age of Diminishing Expectations* (New York: W. W. Norton and Company, Inc., 1979), p. 29.

[5] *Ibid.*, p. 22.

[6] Reinhold Niebuhr, *The Nature and Destiny of Man*, Vol. I (New York: Charles Scribner's Sons, 1941), p. 182.

[7] *Ibid.*, p. 182.

[8] Paul Tillich, *The Courage To Be* (New Haven: Yale University Press, 1952), p. 32.

[9] *Ibid.*, p. 36.

[10] For a more comprehensive view, see Ira Glasser's article "Racism is Alive and Well and Living in Disguise," published in *Christianity and Crisis*, Vol. 41, March 31, 1981.

[11] Lenneal Henderson, Jr., *Public Management.* "Beyond Equity: The Future of Minorities in Urban Management" (June 1982), p. 2.

[12] *Ibid.*, p. 2.

[13] Peter Paris, *The Social Teaching of the Black Church* (Philadelphia: Fortress Press, 1985), p. 28.

Chapter Four

Implications of What the Laity Expect

Although much has been written about the Black church and the Black minister, few studies, if any, have focused exclusively on the urban laity and their expectations of the minister relative to social and political issues. In this connection, this work sought to determine information regarding the laity's expectations of the Black minister in terms of his social and political involvement in the urban condition. Moreover, it was designed to determine if persons who attend the Black church expect the minister to deal with socio-economic and political problems. It was determined that Black church laity expect the minister to be both "priestly" and "activist/political." There was a clear indication that the minister is expected to accommodate a confluence of expectations arising out of a people whose existential situation represents the prototype of polarity and complexity. This partially explains why 78 percent of the respondents expected the minister to be actively concerned for the oppressed, 68.5 percent expected him to be an aggressive political leader and 60.5 percent expected him to give priority to the evangelization of society. Moreover, these findings suggest that the expectations of the laity are multidimensional and cannot be neatly systematized into dichotomous or mutually exclusive categories.

Each of the items (dependent variables) that truly represented social and political statements was interpreted and discussed relative to the responses. Moreover, the chi-square statistic indicated a statistically significant difference in respondents' denomination, income and education and their response to several items. Additionally, the responses to most of the items were favorable such that a majority of the respondents indicated that they expected the minister to be an active social and political leader. Because the Black minister as well as the laity are a part of the same urban environment, the Black urban minister is not afforded the luxury of insouciant passivity because urban problems can only be addressed by understanding their impact on human lives. Compassion for the oppressed is a prerequisite to addressing and eradicating the insidious nature of many social and political problems. In this connection, the laity expect the minister to address areas of inequality, injustice and poverty.

> In 1983, the last recorded year for poverty statistics, the threshold for poverty for a family of four was $10,178.00 according to the standards of the U.S. Bureau of Census. Since the standard was originally defined, it has been increased yearly in order to allow for inflation.[1]

The Black urban minister has the responsibility of not only preaching justice and freedom but participating in the process of transforming these virtuous concepts into actuality. The church must object to jails and prisons overflowing with Blacks. It must actively engage in supporting political movements and politicians that are not only sympathetic to the plight of Blacks but are willing to implement programs that will alter the historical status of Blacks in the system. Joseph R. Washington states,

> The moral and theological basis for the negro church's involvement in politics are not . . . in conflict with or contradiction to the function of the church. Together with the moral requirement to meet the needs of Negroes through a positive acceptance of the masses and their capacity to engage in the challenge of change, the theoretical, theological, moral, and political groundwork is unmistakable.[2]

The Black Church has always been the largest Black owned institution in the Black community. It can at least serve as a meeting place for strategic planning and distributing information to the masses. Furthermore, it can institute educational programs that will help obliterate apathy regarding public policy and the urban condition. In order for this to be done, the Black church needs to listen to the voice of the laity—a voice calling for the engagement of the minister and the church in social and political activities.

> Direct engagement of the Negro church in politics will result not only in a broad base but the much needed injection into the movement of black politics, the hope based upon the Kingdom of God which cannot be shaken by despair. Despair is the inevitable result of hope based upon human beings and institutions. Based on the brotherhood of man demands black politics will be informed by a faith more sustaining, if not more instrumental, than an ideology.[3]

The liberation theology of the Black church must be a practical theology such that it should seek to change the conditions that exist in the community. It can reemphasize self-help, self-determination, freedom, justice, morality and community. This will enable the church to move beyond being a "community of faith" to becoming a conglomerate community concerned not only with faith, but politics, development and the total plight of Black people. The laity expect the minister to be a community leader as well as spiritual leader. Yet, the minister has to internalize these expectations and determine the extent to which his social and political leadership will be determined by the expectations of the laity.

In comparing the results of this study with the results of the national study, it should be noted that the national study by Schuller, Strommen and Brekke, although comprehensive, did not really address the Black urban minister nor the laity's expectations of him from a social and political perspective. The national study focused upon clergy and laity expectations of beginning ministers, while this study only focused upon laity expectations of clergy concerning the social and political arena of ministry in the Black urban community. This study utilized a limited aspect of one major theme in ministry expectations—"Ministry to Community and World." The national study was responsible for the establishment of the categories or areas of ministry and the core clusters that this study used extensively. Additionally, the scope of the national study was so extensive—and this study's scope was so narrow, that comparing them is like comparing apples and oranges. Moreover, this study was limited in its focus as well as its sample because its aim was to deal only with the laity and their expectations of the Black urban minister regarding a specific area of ministry—the social and political. The national study developed the usage of the nomenclature as well as the taxonomy for the areas of ministry, core clusters and the individual items constituting the core clusters. This study is indebted to the Schuller, Strommen and Brekke study for use of one of the eleven areas of ministry—Ministry to Community and World—and three of the core clusters and the items that made up these clusters. Yet, the results of the national study and the results of this study are basically incompatible because of the aforesaid reasons. Additionally, the majority of the respondents in this study were National Baptist or affiliated with the Church of God in Christ; therefore, they had no association with the denominational affiliation of the respondents in the national study (see Appendix E).

Conclusions

1. Denomination made a statistically significant difference in the laity's expectations of clergy on the following variables:
   A. Organizes group to change civil laws which seem in light of scripture to be morally wrong.
   B. Works to integrate people of varying educational, ethnic, and cultural backgrounds into the congregation.
   C. Holds that the church's task of proclaiming the gospel by preaching and teaching overshadows in importance the task of helping to eliminate physical sufferings of people.
2. Education and Income made a statistically significant difference in the laity's expectations of clergy on the following variable: Priorities in use of time indicate the belief that the one and only way to build an ideal world society is to convert everyone to Christianity.

3. Occupation made a statistically significant difference in the laity's expectations of the Black urban minister on the following variables:
   A. Acquaints self with the history and aspirations of minority groups and other oppressed people.
   B. Works to integrate people of varying educational, ethnic, and cultural backgrounds into the congregation.
4. Denomination did not make a statistically significant difference in the laity's overall social and political expectations of the Black urban minister.
5. Socio-economic status did not make a statistically significant difference in the laity's overall social and political expectation of the Black urban minister.
6. A majority of persons in this study had income over $21,000. Moreover, the largest percentage of respondents, 33.1 percent, had income of $27,000 and above.
7. The majority of the respondents in this study had attended college while 15.7 percent were college graduates.
8. The highest percentage of the respondents were Baptist and female—36.1 percent and 71.3 percent respectively.

The conclusions of this study suggest that the Black urban minister has a constituency that will support his active involvement on behalf of the oppressed as well as his providing aggressive political leadership in the urban community. Moreover, Black laity seem to be quite homogenous in the expectations of the minister such that denomination and socio-economic status do not affect the overall expectations of the Black church constituency.

Limitations

This study was limited to three hundred and thirty-eight respondents in one southeastern Virginia city. It was also confined to Black church laity who were basically unassociated with the Association of Theological Schools in America and Canada. This contributed to its uniqueness while simultaneously disenabling any substantive comparison with the national study.

This book resulted from a survey that was developed by the Association of Theological Schools in America and Canada to gather information nationally from its affiliated schools and churches in order to determine clergy and laity expectations of beginning ministers. A portion of that survey was used in this study to determine laity expectations of clergy. While the validity of the survey is not questioned, the use of only a segment of it was a limitation of this study from a comparative perspective.

Moreover, because the writer could not secure the permission of several ministers in order to administer the survey in their churches, other churches whose pastors were more cooperative, had to be chosen. This limitation vis-a-vis the fact that some persons present at the churches during the administration of the survey refused to participate, was expected but, could not be avoided.

Overall, this study proceeded according to plan.

Implications

Many implications for urban management can be made from this study because the Black church and its constituents are a major part of the urban environment. "City governments today stand amidst a host of pressures and conflicts and successful urban managers must develop an understanding of these myriad external forces."[4] The Black church laity is one of many external forces that characterize urban America. Moreover, the Black church is an integral part of the urban milieu such that a coalescing of the somewhat latent force that is inherent in the numerical and political strength of the Black church laity has the potential ability to change the face of urban America.

> Since the turmoil of the sixties, however, city governments have found it necessary to shift their attention from physical and technical concerns to human problems. In particular, urban public leadership increasingly has been called on to provide justice and services for those whose needs are greatest— the poor, the old and handicapped and the *subjects of ethnic and racial discrimination.*[5]

Our research found that the laity expected the minister to be actively concerned about the plight of the oppressed and to provide political leadership in the community; therefore, specific implications of our research have been divided into three areas—ministerial, laity and church/state.

1. Black ministers in urban areas should actively seek political office. This will enable them to actively participate in the political process.
2. Black ministers need to value the opinions of their constituents—the laity. This means that after the minister attains a political position, he should use that position to advance the plight of the poor and minorities. He should risk becoming a gadfly (in the Socratic sense) in order that the voice "from down under" will be heard.
3. The laity clearly expect the minister to be socially and politically active. Nevertheless, this demands time and other resources that few ministers have because many already have second jobs. What is the laity willing to do in order to accommodate their own expectations of the minister? Are the persons, who expect the minister to be both socially and politically active as well as evangelistic, willing to support an increase in the church's staff in order that the minister can do more of the things that are expected?
4. Inasmuch as the Black urban laity expect the minister to be socially and politically active in the community, does this suggest that there will be a corresponding level of activity on their part? If the expectations of the laity reflect an inherent interest by them to augment or complement the efforts of the minister, then a collaborative effort by both groups has the potential to transform the urban environment.
5. The national issue of church and state or politics and religion, highlighted in the 1984 presidential campaign, seems to be a nebulous one in the eyes of the Black church laity because they expect the minister to synchronize these two concepts such that the problems of oppression and injustice in the urban milieu will be addressed from a political and religious perspective. For the Black laity, there is no absolute polarity

between the pragmatic use of politics and religion. The Black church laity understand that the church and the state are already intimately aligned. For example, protestant marriages are performed by clergy after the state grants a license to the parties involved. Is marriage a church or state function? This example suggests that the dichotomy between church and state or politics and religion is more perceived than real—more ideal than practical. Historically, the Black laity understand that slavery was not just a state institution sanctioned by law, but that the church (religion) corroborated its intent and collaborated in maintaining its sacrosanctity by biblically "substantiating" its virtues. The eradication of oppression and injustice, however biblically based, presents society with a political (state) dilemma.

6. Some questions have been raised by this study. Some of them are the following:

   A. Would this study have been more compatible with the national study had it sought to determine laity and clergy expectations of ministers using all of the core clusters constituting "Ministry to Community and World"?

   B. Would a larger sample of the Black church laity (constituting several area cities) have yielded the same results?

   C. What types of persons did not complete the survey? Was the population of the churches, on the particular Sunday of the survey, representative of the normal attendance of these churches?

   D. How are expectations of laity conveyed to the minister? And, once expectations are known, how do they correlate with actual performance?

Suggestions for Future Research

Some suggestions for future research are listed below:

1. A comparison of White and Black expectations of the urban minister vis-a-vis social and political issues would clearly

establish the similarities and differences between Black and White laity expectations. This study could focus upon a particular urban area or region.

2. The National Study conducted by the Association of Theological Schools in America and Canada should be duplicated in the Black urban church in America in order to determine some general and specific differences between clergy and laity expectations of beginning ministers.

3. The impact of the Black urban church upon the stability of the nuclear family. Inasmuch as the church is a staple of the Black community, this research will determine how it (the church) positively affects the Black family as a social unit.

FOOTNOTES

[1] Steve Suitts, *Patterns of Poverty: A Special Report of the Southern Regional Council* (Atlanta: The Southern Regional Council, 1984), p. 12.

[2] Hart M. Nelson, Raytha L. Yokley and Anne K. Nelson, eds., *The Black Church in America* (New York: Basic Books, Inc., 1971), p. 303.

[3] *Ibid.*, p. 307.

[4] David R. Morgan, *Managing Urban America* (North Scituate, Mass.: Duxbury Press, 1979), p. 12.

[5] *Ibid.*, p. 15.

Chapter Five

An Essay on Sources

*"... justice is the first condition required
for the existence of the city."*
—St. Augustine

The study of urban laity and clergy demands some understanding of theology simply because the church and theology are inherently interconnected. In recent years, there has been an increasing number of persons who have questioned the foundation and values of what is generally termed "traditional theology" and refocused their energies on the establishment of a philosophy or theology of liberation. These theories of liberation theology within the Christian context are grounded in experiential phenomena that perceive the situation of the poor and oppressed as the result of domination and systematic injustice. Moreover, the moral and ethical mandate of liberation theology manifests itself in active pursuit of an equitable society and in inculcating the ideals of freedom, justice, love and reconciliation into the fabric of the community. In this connection, the sensitivity of clergy and laity to the social and political ills that are endemic to urban America can be enhanced through understanding the essence of liberation theology.

Perspectives on Liberation

Gustavo Gutierrez, the South American Theologian, is adept in understanding the suffering of the poor and oppressed. In *A Theology of Liberation*, he attempts to dissect the meaning of liberation and suggests that it is a process inherently connected to the salvific work of Jesus Christ. Gutierrez was one of the earliest Latin American writers on liberation theology probably because of his existential situation. The people of Latin America are indeed victims of exploitation and oppression. Gutierrez's later work, *Liberation and Change*, written in conjunction with Robert Shaull, is appropriately subtitled "Freedom and Salvation—A Political Problem." In this work, he renders a thorough explication of freedom and indicates that the theology of liberation is an indigenous theology such that the Latin American experience of poverty and the struggle to attain freedom substantiates its uniqueness. Yet, liberation theology is not confined to geographic boundaries. It is based on experiences of injustice and oppression such that persons who live outside of the boundaries of South America may experience an equal or greater level of oppression. Therefore, we have Blacks and women who have developed theologies of liberation—especially James Cone (*A Black Theology of Liberation*) and Rosemary Ruether (*Liberation Theology*).

Jurgen Moltmann deals with the psychological and political liberation of people in an effort to move toward a hermeneutic of liberation from these perspectives. He writes,

> What is needed here is therefore a psychological hermeneutics of the word of the cross, the spirit of freedom and the history of God. Psychological hermeneutics is an interpretation and not a reduction. Like political hermeneutics, it is a translation of the theological langugage of liberation by a particular dimension of life.[1]

In an attempt to show some correlation between the dialectic of law and freedom in traditional Christian theology and pathology/therapy, Moltmann talks of a psychological hermeneutic. In this connection, Moltmann states,

> Concrete attention must be paid to religious problems of politics and to laws, compulsion and the vicious circle which for economic and social reasons,

> constrict, oppress, or make impossible the life of man
> and living humanity. . . . The freedom of faith
> therefore urges men on towards liberating actions,
> because it makes them painfully aware of suffering in
> situations of exploitation, oppression, alienation and
> captivity.[2]

Political hermeneutics visualizes the barriers that exist between man and man in connection with the structures of deprivation that contribute to inhumanity. Furthermore, Moltmann makes it clear that political hermeneutics questions the sense of God talk vis-a-vis the prevailing social and economic conditions of man.

> Political hermeneutics sets out to recognize the
> social and economic influences on theological insti-
> tutions and languages in order to bring their lib-
> erating content into the political dimension and to
> make them relevant towards really freeing men from
> their misery in certain vicious circles. . . . Christian
> theology must be politically clear whether it is
> disseminating faith or superstition.[3]

If Christian Theology is disseminating faith, then it must internalize and disseminate a message that corresponds to the life of Jesus and the means by which he arrived on the cross. Ernst Kasemann calls Jesus a "liberal" but Moltmann calls him a "rebel." Indeed he was crucified because he rebelled against the authorities, tradition and the law. His accusers charged him with blasphemy because he essentially put himself in God's stead. He neither looked nor acted in a way to confirm the authenticity of his Messiahship in accordance with the expectations of the authorities. By acting the way he did, "Jesus placed his preaching of God, and therefore himself, above the authority of Moses and the Torah."[4] It is evident that Jesus was in conflict with the religious leaders of his day regarding the interpretation of the law. Accordingly, the label "blasphemer" can be understood. Also, his rejection and punishment for the crime of blasphemy can be legally understood but his execution by crucifixion is inconsistent.

> Jesus did not undergo the punishment for blas-
> phemy, which in Israel at this time, as can be seen by
> the death of Stephen, was always stoning. Jesus was

crucified by the Roman occupying power.[5]

The inference derived from this action clearly suggests that Jesus was perceived by the authorities as a political activist—a rebel in conflict with the ideology of the state.

> Crucifixion was a punishment for crimes against the state, and not part of general criminal jurisdiction. To this extent, one can say that crucifixion at that time was a political punishment for rebellion against the social and political order of the Imperium Romanum.[6]

The death of Jesus shows that there is no simple distinction between religion and politics; and Moltmann takes issue with Rudolph Bultmann who speaks of Jesus' activity as "being misconstrued as political activity."[7] For Moltmann, religion is not a private matter and has never been (refer to Jesus' crucifixion) because it often threatens others.

In the hermeneutical scheme of Moltmann, the liberation of individuals must be seen in light of the cross. It is the reality of the cross that allows us to conceptualize Jesus as an oppressed and humiliated being. The cross as a symbol of unmerited suffering allows Liberation Theology to express itself in relation to this culminating event in the life of the historical Jesus, the crucified God. "The crucified God is in fact a stateless and classless God. But, that does not mean that he is an unpolitical God. He is the God of the poor, the oppressed and humiliated."[8] The political aspects of the crucifixion are relevant to liberation theology because the situation of the life and death of Jesus is directly related to the social and political structures of that day. Whenever the law is changed unjustly or ignored in order to accommodate the desires of those who wield power, then the law becomes engulfed in politics. Indeed, the death of Jesus was such that the punishment was not consistent with the crime.

> Now the death of Christ was the death of a political offender. According to the scale of social values of the time, crucifixion was dishonour and shame. If this crucified man has been raised from the dead, and exhalted to be the Christ of God, then what public opinion holds to be the lowliest, what the state has determined to be disgraceful, is changed into what is

supreme. In that case, the glory of God does not
shine on the crown of the mighty, but on the face of
the crucified Christ. The authority of God is then no
longer represented directly by those in high positions, the powerful and the rich, but by the outcast
Son of Man, who died between two Wretches.[9]

Those in society who have been treated as outcasts are
experiential descendants of Jesus. Moreover, the method used to
bring about the death of Jesus was identical to that used for
exterminating criminals. The cruel and debase nature of the
crucifixion as experienced by Jesus, and indeed to the Christian, is
the chief example of historical injustice. Liberation Theology, when
viewed in light of the cross, represents a parallel between those who
suffer from present conditions of unfreedom, oppression and
injustice and the suffering and death of Christ on the cross.

The social and political activities of the sixties performed by
clergy and laity are examples of the quest for liberation. The fact that
the Black church was in the forefront of this social movement
suggests that an active political ministry has historically characterized Black clergy and laity. Moreover, there has been a consistent
parallel between the suffering of Jesus and the suffering of Blacks in
America.

The situation of Blacks in America has been marked by efforts
to negate their ontology. Slavery, the Three-Fifths Clause and the
Dred Scott decision of 1857 are primary examples of an effort to
reduce Blacks to the status of non-beings. These efforts are well
documented in the annals of American history. Moreover, they
suggest a systematic and conscious effort by the leaders of a nation
which based its Constitution and Declaration of Independence on
the ideals of freedom and justice. Yet, Ralph Ellison captures the
spirit of struggle.

I am an invisible man. No, I am not a spook like those
who haunted Edgar Allan Poe; nor am I one of your
Hollywood-movie ectoplasms. . . . I am a man of
substance, of flesh and bone, fiber and liquids—and I
might even be said to possess a mind. I am invisible,
understand, simply because people refuse to see me.

Like the bodiless heads you see sometimes in circus sideshows, it is as though I have been surrounded by mirrors of hard, distorting glass. When they approach me, they see only my surroundings, themselves or figments of their imagination — indeed everything and anything except me.[10]

Liberation Theology seeks to give visibility to those who are not seen. Not only must Black clergy and laity be seen, but they must be heard with a new openness, because the experience of Blacks cannot be denied.

Speak the truth to the people
Talk sense to the people
Free them with reason
Free them with honesty
Free the people with love and
courage and care for their being . . .[11]

Freedom is indeed the essence of Liberation Theology as seen from the Black perspective and the sources and norm of this theology are grounded in experiences. "That is, the sources are the relevant data for the theological task, while the norm determines how the data will be used."[12] The task is to create an environment of freedom where the Black clergy would serve as a catalyst in dismantling the social and political barriers that prevent equality in urban areas. In Black Theology, an effort has been made to make God talk relevant to the past and present situation of existence in the Black community. Inasmuch as traditional theology has dealt with issues that ultimately are of little practical value to those who are oppressed; Black Theology seeks to speak to God as He relates to the existential sitution of Black people. Cone states that "the source of Black Theology must be consistent with the perspective of the Black community."[13] He systematically lists as sources of Black Theology the following: (1) Black experience, (2) Black History, (3) Black Culture, (4) Revelation, (5) Scripture and (6) Tradition. Each of these sources contributes to the nature of understanding the Black man in terms of his blackness. The writer suggests that Cone's list of sources is quite exhaustive and is overlapping. The overlapping nature of Black experience, Black History and Black Culture can be enmeshed into one category, "the black experience." In the same connection, Revelation, Scripture and Tradition can be enmeshed to form Scripture/Tradition.

With the Black Experience and Scripture/Tradition, the past and the present can be totally encompassed.

Secondly, the norm in Black Theology is Jesus Christ.

> The theological norm is the hermeneutical principle which is decisive in specifying how sources are to be used by noting their importance and by distinguishing the relevant data from the irrelevant.[14]

Christocentric History and Black Liberation

Indeed, the slaves would sing of Jesus as the source of hope and strength and today the Christocentric nature of worship in the Black Church still exists. The spiritual or Black folksong, "Steal Away . . . to Jesus," continues to represent Jesus as the focus of Black practical religion.

In a related connection, Black Theology interprets the Exodus experience as recorded in the Old Testament as a parallel to the Black Experience.

> The exodus was the decisive event in Israel's history, because through it Yahweh revealed himself as the Savior of an oppressed people. The Israelites were slaves in Egypt; thus their future was closed. But . . . Yahweh, therefore, took Israel's history into his own hands and gave his people a divine future thereby doing for Israel what she could not do for herself.[15]

In the Exodus experience or event, God shows forth his power and favor toward the oppressed.

> God's election of the oppressed Israelites have unavoidable implications for the doing of theology. If God had chosen as his 'holy nation' the Egyptian slave masters instead of the Israelite slaves, then a completely different kind of God would have been revealed. Thus Israel's election cannot be separated from her servitude and liberation. Here God discloses that he is the God of history whose will is identical with the liberation of the oppressed from

social and political bondage.[16]

The vindication of the weak from the forces of the strong is apparent in the Exodus story and in the covenant established between Yahweh and Israel which shows the "specialness" of this people in the sight of God. It must also be understood that when the Israelites forgot about the grace and kindness of God and became "other than" what God expected of them, then they too were chastised. "According to Amos and Hosea, Israel will be punished because the people do not practice loyalty and justice."[17] When the poor of the Lord were forgotten and injustice was rampant in Israel, the prophet Amos speaks the sentiments of God by declaring,

> You trample the poor and force him to give you grain. Therefore, though you have built stone mansions, you will not live in them, though you have planted lush vineyards, you will not drink their wine. For I know how many are your offenses and how great your sins.[18]

The most prolific of Amos' prophet discourses against Israel's injustice is capsuled in his reference to the day of the Lord which Israel had longed for—"Why do you long for the Lord?" he asks. Such questions show their ignorance of their own actions and their inability to realize God's disappointment with them.

> I hate, I despise your religious feasts; I cannot stand your assemblies. Even though you bring me burnt offerings and grain offerings, I will not accept them. Though you bring choice fellowship offerings, I will not accept them. Away with the noise of your songs! I will not listen to the music of your harps. But let justice roll on like a river, righteousness like a never failing streat![19]

These words are quite harsh; yet, they show that God is extremely concerned with justice and hates the calm, nonchalant disinterest of those who worship with a prevailing and persistent apathy toward the presence of injustice and unrighteousness. Cone states,

> It is a fact! In almost every scene of the Old Testament drama of salvation, the poor are defended against the rich, the weak against the strong. Yahweh

is the God of the oppressed whose revelation is
identical with their liberation from bondage. Even in
the wisdom literature where the sages seem to be
unaware of Israel's saving history, God's concern for
the poor is nonetheless emphasized.[20]

From this liberation perspective, God is insulted by oppression and a true understanding of his interest in the poor is to hear his word with a new openness. "He who oppresses the poor insults his maker; he who is generous to the needy honors him."[21]

The message of freedom does not end with the Old Testament but is personified in Jesus Christ. "Jesus means freedom" in the practical sense of the word. Moreover, Jesus symbolically means to live in freedom from oppression and injustice. The freedom to be free is the mandate of any kerygmatic understanding of the Good news.

The spirit of the Lord is upon me, because he has
anointed me to preach good news to the poor. He has
sent me to proclaim freedom for the prisoner and
recovery of sight for the blind, to release the oppressed, to proclaim the year of the Lord's favor.[22]

To be a man is to be fully human such that one's humanity is not deprived nor impinged upon to the extent that inhuman treatment becomes the norm. Such ideology, upon implementation, obliterates true manhood and perpetuates a distorted view of humanity. Until the freedom of all men becomes a concern and a goal of all men, the tensions and rebellions that exist between man and man cannot begin to cease.

The image of Blacks in America is "colored" by the fact that they were once chattel property. Other images have been perpetrated by aberrant behavior and actions. The painful process of overcoming bestowed images is long and arduous. Moreover, it is the image of the Black man which is embraced by the majority that tends to pervade the social and religious structures of society.

The story of the Negro in America is . . . not a pretty
story: The story of a people is never very pretty. . . .
He is a series of shadows, self created, intertwining,
which now we helplessly battle. One may say that the
Negro in America does not really exist except in the
darkness of our minds. . . . To think of him is to

think of statistics, slums, rapes, injustice, remote violence. . . .[23]

Such bestowed images are the product of a massive imagination that works to enhance ingrained concepts of the Black man as something less than human—therefore, less than free and capable or desiring self-determination. Blacks in America have survived against the odds. The process of overcoming systematic oppression historically, e.g., slavery, the three-fifths constitutional clause and other legal barriers have given impetus to the quest for freedom and justice. Contrary to these images, the heart of the biblical understanding of man is centered around the 'image' of God in man."[24] Yet, the iamge of the Black man by Whites historically has been characterized by adjectives such as lazy, shiftless, inferior—"less than." James Deotis Roberts quotes H. Shelton Smith who writes, "Southern religion from 1780 to 1910 was notorious for distorting the biblical understanding of man in order to support slavery and racism."[25] The politics of religion were definitely involved in the relationship between salvation and freedom as it related to slavery. Pauline Theology (cf. Col. 3:22 and Philemon), was the "proof text" par excellence for maintaining that slavery was biblically justified. Therefore, Blacks could be held in physical bondage and simultaneously be free "in Christ." Dr. Roberts makes this contradiction clearer by stating,

> They had to deal with a legal question that has a socio-economic base, the question as to whether salvation and freedom from slavery are related. This was settled in a negative statement by a Virginia court; conversion and emancipation do not take place at the same time. Only theological endorsement remained necessary to make this position acceptable to church and state. In law, custom and theology, we have the position established that the Black man is only partly human.[26]

Liberation theology recognizes that vestiges of the slavery mentality still exist and such a mentality is a gross distortion of the reality of Black existence.

The relationship between the "Imago Dei" and existential

freedom has not captured the attention of traditional or historical theology. "In the history of theology, the image of God is generally conceived of as man's rationality and freedom."[27] Yet "freedom" is obscured because it has little or no reference to the oppressed. "It is significant that freedom and rational reflection go hand in hand, without connection to the rebellion of the oppressed."[28] In Liberation theology, freedom is not a philosophical issue to be debated until it meets its demise in abstraction. But it is experiential.

Freedom "in Christ" or "in the spirit" does not compensate (for) nor alleviate oppression. "Freedom is not a rational decision about possible alternatives; it is a participation of the whole man in the liberation struggle."[29]

Liberation theology recognizes the existential situation of Black people—an existence bordering on despair. Yet, the hope of deliverance never fades into oblivion because Black people do not believe that "God expected them to be 'hewers of wood and drawers of water' as some devout churchgoers in white skin sincerely believe."[30] Black people cannot truly exist except in freedom to be truly free and finally bring to past the historic words stated in jubilation by Martin Luther King, Jr.—"Free at last, Free at last, Thank God Almighty, I'm free at last!"

Laity expectations of clergy in urban areas as they relate to social and political involvement can be better understood within this theoretical framework. Because liberation requires active involvement in the social and political life of the community, the laity's expectations of the clergy in this connection will help to confirm or deny their interest in liberation. In other words, if the Black laity expect the clergy to be involved in the active alleviation of poverty, high unemployment and the host of other atrocities that plague the urban milieu, then said expectations will be tantamount to admission of a desire for clergy involvement.

Social and political involvement is the means by which liberation is effectuated; laity expectations and the concept of liberation are interrelated when we are concerned about ministry to the whole community. Even during biblical times, religiously inspired political activities varied. Clearly, the prophets, i.e., Amos, Jeremiah and

Hosea, as well as Jesus Christ, offer models for politically and socially active ministry.

Clergy, Laity and the Urban Milieu

Ministry in urban areas cannot be confined to traditional ecclesiastical actions or expectations. Moreover, the realities of poverty, poor housing and high unemployment among Blacks are representative of problems that generally are not addressed by the traditional role of the clergy. In an urban society, ministry is a social and political phenomenon that addresses the prevailing ills of the cities. To this end, the minister focuses his attention. Therefore, many of the social realities that result in inequities as well as the political realities that facilitate and accommodate these conditions become the focus of ministry to the community.

The most recent study that analyzes the expectations of clergy and laity relative to ministry in a way that reflects the urban condition as well as other facets of ministry is entitled *Ministry In America*. This study, sponsored by the Association of Theological Schools in America and Canada, utilizes a national random sample of 5,000 clergy and laity, in rating 444 descriptions of ministry which were statistically combined into 64 clusters using cluster analysis and factor analysis. This epoch making study asserts that "laypeople, as a special rule, place far less importance than do clergy on ministries outside of the congregation."[31] The study did not seek to ascertain only the laity's expectations of clergy, but clergy expectations of clergy as well. Furthermore, it offers valuable information in understanding ministry as it relates to the community and world which is crucial to clarifying expectations by the laity. There were eleven major areas of ministry perceived as most important in this particular study; but, the area of relevance to the urban condition concerns the community and the larger environment.

The most important area of ministry in the Schuller, Strommen and Brekke study that relates to the focus of this writer's study is "Ministry to the Community and World." They describe this theme by stating that,

> 'Ministry to Community and World' portrays a ministry area of aggressive political leadership coupled with an active concern for the oppressed. It is an area of ministry characterized by openness to new ideas and in personal style and giving pastoral service to all people. Respondents who see this theme as highly important are endorsing activities such as 'works to improve community service to older people. . . . Insists that political struggle is a rightful concern of the church.' The theme clearly identifies an area of ministry that is socially conscious, issue-oriented, concerned for the oppressed and actively seeking to rectify social injustices—particularly by means of political action.[32]

Political action and social action are necessitated by environmental realities in urban communities. Only abject detachment enables persons to minister in the midst of suffering without being affected by it. In urban areas, suffering and pain are the results of various social ills.

> People in political ministry accept their responsibility for changing these (social, economic and political) systems, for getting at the roots of injustice. They believe that the systems are potentially transformable, and that political action is an effective tool. For this reason they focus their energy on legislation, believing that reorienting public policy is a force for incremental systematic change. . . . It is a way to move step by step from how society is now to a preferred world. It enables people to be practical about their vision. As they attend to what is possible now—immediate, effective structural changes—they also move toward eventual overall systematic change. Their activity is more than reform, a minimization of injustice in existing structures. It is an attempt to restructure society itself.[33]

While persons who constitute a formal religious lobby are involved in political and social ministry, the Black urban minister, however inadvertently, finds himself involved also in political problems.

The study by Schuller, Stommen and Brekke, *Ministry in America*, although comprehensive, fails to treat Black laity or clergy as a distinct group basically because it is based on responses from persons associated with the Association for Theological Schools in America and Canada. This is a limitation not in scope but in specificity. Even though random sampling was used in administering the questionnaire, the majority of Black clergy and laity are not associated with ATS. Furthermore, association with ATS implies that clergy are involved in theological education. The fact that only a small percentage of all Black clergy have been seminary trained renders its generalizability to Black clergy and laity suspect. The authors indicate the limitations by stating that,

> A second limitation resides in the fact that this study was carried out through the 200 seminaries in the Association of Theological Schools in the United States and Canada. Hence, the samples were limited to (1) denominations that had one or more seminaries in the professional accrediting association; (2) clergy who were seminary trained, which in the case of the Southern Baptist eliminated almost one half of its clergy; and (3) laity who were members of congregations served by clergy trained in a member seminary of ATS. As a result, the random samples exclude portions of the religious community whose seminaries are not accredited, whose clergy are not seminary trained and whose laity are found in congregations led by pastors without seminary training.[34]

From a practical perspective, the limitations of the aforesaid study, in effect, exclude the majority of Black laity as well as clergy. The study that this writer conducted was not subject to the aforesaid limitations because the focus was placed on laity expectations without regard to training of the pastor and therefore, without regard to ties with ATS. This is important, relative to ministry in the Black church because,

> Recent figures show that only one out of fifteen men entering the ministry has had seminary training. In other words, 92 percent of the men entering the Negro Ministry each year are professionally unprepared.[35]

Because this study focused only on Black laity expectations of clergy in urban areas, it has served a need not met in any previous study. A further caution needs to be mentioned about the Schuller, Strommen and Brekke study. Their study was basically concerned with expectations of ministers immediately after completion of seminary training. The limitations, as indicated earlier, will not be imposed on our study. Moreover, the limitations of the Schuller, Strommen and Brekke study are expressed best in their own words. They write,

> Unfortunately, we were unable to secure responses from a sufficient number of Black clergy and laity to warrant separate analysis and reporting. Each Black respondent consequently has been totaled within his/her own denominational group. Because an empirical analysis of responses of those in the African Methodist Episcopal Zion Church showed greatest affiliation with the larger family of the Presbyterian-Reformed Church, their data were included in that denominational family.[36]

Because there is a uniqueness surrounding the position of Blacks in urban areas relative to the conditions of the community, the laity are a potential determinant of change. Recently, the *Washington Post* in reporting on the 67th annual convocation of Howard University School of Divinity indicated that Black pastors are losing authority to the laity.

> Historically, before the elections of black mayors in many cities, pastors served as 'mayors' of their communities and were powerful leaders whose word often was taken as gospel by churchgoers. . . . Now, 'the congregations are asking for a piece of the pie.'[37]

This is indicative of the importance of the laity in the Black church and their expectations of the minister. Given the fact that the minister's schedule and responsibilities are burdensome, the laity may expect the minister to delegate more responsibilities to them as was indicated by the sentiment at the Howard University Conference.

> One remedy for pastors is to begin delegating more authority to lay persons within the church . . . especially on nonministerial matters such as political

awareness meetings, which they said was a primary
challenge for the Black church in the 1980's. . . . In
years past . . . Black churches dealt with Jim Crow
laws and civil rights issues. Now unemployment . . .
and increased poverty among Blacks have emerged
as critical church issues.[38]

The fact that unemployment and increased poverty are seen as
"church issues" implies that the laity are concerned. Furthermore,
Milloy's article quoted above entitled "Black Pastors Seen Losing
Authority to Congregations" is somewhat a misnomer because the
laity have always had considerable authority especially in the non-
hierarchical churches which constitute the majority of Black people
participating in the Black church.[39]

Social and political issues are an intricate part of the fabric of
urban America. And, in some cases, while the laity may have
expectations of the minister, he does not always address the pressing
social and political problems. In "The Sounds of Silence Revisited,"
Norman Koller and Joseph D. Retzer reexamine findings of an earlier
study "Sounds of Silence" which concluded that most clergy don't
speak out on issues of controversy. Specifically, "the research team
concluded that, in spite of the heated political and social climate of
the time (1960's), most clergy were reluctant to speak out on social
issues."[40] This study, done some ten years later (1980) focused on a
sample from North Carolina as compared to California. A questionnaire was mailed to 468 Protestant Ministers in two southwestern
counties of North Carolina. There was a 99.6 percent response rate.
Unlike the earlier findings, this study found that:

> Nearly all respondents expressed a high level of
> interest in social and political issues. Ninety-four
> percent agreed with the statement, 'I am interested in
> the contemporary social and political issues in cur-
> rent American society.'[41]

In the same study, the authors state,

> In considering the clergy's role in social issues, 84
> percent reported that their theological training en-
> couraged them to speak out on social and political
> issues. Ninety percent felt it to be their duty to speak
> out in the community, and fully 82 percent felt they

should do so in sermons.[42]

The relationship between theological training and speaking out on social issues is not clearly established. Inasmuch as a small percentage of Black ministers have formal theological education, it is evident that something other than theological education influences their involvement. Many voices who have spoken and continue to speak out are informed by experiential compulsion rather than theological hermeneutics. The Schuller, Strommen and Brekke study had a limited number of Blacks in their sample and even fewer responses—although the responses were weighted. Moreover, the assertion by Charles Hamilton that 92 percent of Black ministers do not have formal theological training seems to discount the significance of any causal relationship between theological training and social and political involvement. This does not suggest that there is a negative correlation between the aforesaid variables but rather indicates that there is limited generalizability of findings that suggest a positive relationship between theological training and social and political involvement.

Moreover, education in the broadest sense is a political phenomenon, and educated Blacks are often quite active politically and socially.

> What we are pointing out is that the increased political activity on the part of Black Americans is a part of their Black Religious Experience in this country. That political activity is a part of that drive, that urge toward freedom and liberation. It is a part of the quest for a rhythm of life, a place in which everything has a place. It is a quest for change to be sure. However, it is also a quest for meaning. It is a quest to make sense out of nonsense.[43]

Historically, political activity has been a part of the structure of the religious experience for Blacks. During the same year Thomas Jefferson was elected President of the United States, slave revolts began. This was in 1800 and the rebellion of the participants in the Black church to the dehumanizing reality of slavery began to take form. Gayraud Wilmore states,

> A young man of twenty-five named Gabriel, slave of

Thomas Prosser, whose plantation was just outside
of the City of Richmond, Virginia, was moved to
strike the first blow for liberty in the new century. A
man of impressive physical and mental capacities,
Gabriel was also a student of the Bible and was
strongly drawn to lead an insurrection among the
slaves by religious convictions.[44]

The political activity of Gabriel Prosser, Denmark Vessey and
Nat Turner was in some way related to the Black church. In this
connection, Marshall Grigsby is correct in pointing out that political
activity has historically engulfed Black religion by way of minister and
laity. Nat Turner, Denmark Vessey and Gabriel Prosser were
ministers-leaders with deep religious convictions about freedom
such that they were willing to give their lives as a sacrifice to the ideal
of liberation. They brought people together for a meaningful cause.

Because the Schuller, Strommen and Brekke study facilitated
this study's design, it was necessary to extrapolate the areas of
importance in order to clarify this particular project. Their pre-
liminary study, *Readiness For Ministry, Vols. 1 & 2,* culminated in the
book, *Ministry in America.* Out of the 5,000 persons who responded
to the questionnaire, the authors were able to form factors for each
separate theme in the core clusters (after homogeneous clustering
and factor analysis were performed).

The result was sixty-four core clusters which factored into
eleven major themes. The core clusters are formed by similar
responses to items in the entire questionnaire. As indicated previously, we focused on one of the eleven major themes, i.e., "Ministry
to Community and World" which consists of nine clusters (as
indicated in the Schuller, Strommen and Brekke study). Therefore,
our research used the items from the Schuller, et al. questionnaire
that are constitutive of the major area—"Ministry to Community and
World." The fact that our questionnaire was administered only to
minorities in a specified urban area has presented a clearer
description of how Black urban church participants (laity) perceive
these criteria as they relate to expectations of ministers. Furthermore, a general (nonstatistical) and limited comparison of the sample
responses in this study was made with the results achieved in the

national study in order to identify differences in expectations of the national sample and the local sample on specific items in the survey. We discussed this in Chapter 4.

Moreover, we purposely chose three of the core clusters from the ten that constituted ministry to community and world because they were uniquely constitutive of the elements that this book addressed.

Summary

Before and since the Revolutionary War era, Black clergy have been impelled by a relentless quest to be free. Richard Allen, Absolom Jones and James Varick were early leaders of a movement that rejected oppression in the White church and society and culminated in the establishment of a church for Blacks. This independent Black church movement, during that period, was an expression of Black resistance to oppression—the first Black freedom movement. This movement coincided with the American Revolutionary War and the drafting and ratification of the Constitution of the United States. These founders of Black churches and mutual aid societies were the religious leaders of that time. They also provided the impetus for impacting upon the social and political structures of an era laden with injustice. In reality, these persons established the institutions that have been at variance with oppression and remain at the forefront of social and political activism. Indeed these institutions, especially the Black church, produced many of the prominent leaders of the sixties and, the most effective Black leader in dealing with eradicating the vestiges of the pre-civil war era and striking down legal and social barriers to freedom was Martin Luther King, Jr., a product of the Black church. The many accomplishments of Black clergy have generally been attributed to them and not to the force of the laity. The urban centers of the south and northeast were the battlegrounds of social change. The force for much of this change was born in and sustained by the Black church laity. This is justifiable, but this study sought to determine the relationship between laity expectations regarding social and political involvement and the actual involvement of the minister. It is not clear whether socially and politically active ministers are responding to an internal compulsion or an external force—namely, the laity. Moreover, a combination of both forces is highly probable.

Liberation theology is a system of understanding God-talk that realistically faces the facts of urban existence such that, poverty, population decline, housing inadequacies, racism and injustice are not perceived as separate and apart from the task of ministering. Ministry to the community and world involves an effort to address and change the prevailing social and political conditions in urban areas. Liberation and Black theology offer a means by which this effort can be understood and a framework for achieving these changes.

FOOTNOTES

[1] Jurgen Moltmann, *The Crucified God* (New York: Harper and Row, 1974), p. 292.

[2] *Ibid.*, p. 317.

[3] *Ibid.*, p. 318.

[4] *Ibid.*, p. 128.

[5] *Ibid.*, p. 136.

[6] *Ibid.*

[7] *Ibid.*, p. 137.

[8] *Ibid.*, p. 329.

[9] *Ibid.*, p. 327.

[10] Ralph Ellison, *The Invisible Man* (New York: Random House, 1952), p. 3.

[11] James H. Cone, *God of the Oppressed* (New York: The Seabury Press, Inc., 1975), p. 16.

[12] *Ibid.*, p. 51.

13 James H. Cone, *A Black Theology of Liberation* (New York: J.B. Lippincott Co., 1970), p. 53.

14 *Ibid.*, p. 75.

15 Cone, *God of the Oppressed*, p. 63.

16 *Ibid.*, p. 65.

17 *Ibid.*, p. 67.

18 Amos 5:11-12 (NIV).

19 Amos 5:21-24 (NIV).

20 Cone, *God of the Oppressed*, p. 70.

21 Proverbs 14:13 (NEB).

22 Luke

23 Abraham Chapman, ed., *Black Voices: An Anthology of Afro-American Literature* (New York: The New English Library Ltd., 1968), p. 590-1.

24 J. Deotis Roberts, *A Black Political Theology* (Philadelphia: The Westminster Press, 1974), p. 76.

25 *Ibid.*, p. 74.

26 *Ibid.*, p. 76.

27 Cone, *A Black Theology of Liberation*, p. 64.

28 *Ibid.*, p. 165.

29 *Ibid.*, p. 168.

30 Roberts, *A Black Political Theology*, p. 92.

31 David Schuller, Merton Strommen and Milo Brekke, eds., *Ministry in America* (San Francisco: Harper and Row, 1980), p. 70.

32 *Ibid.*, p. 43.

33 Ronald Pasquariello, Donald W. Shriver and Alan Geyer, eds.,

Redeeming the City: Theology Politics and Urban Policy (New York: The Pilgrim Press, 1982), p. 154.

34 Schuller, *Ministry In America*, p. xxi.

35 Charles V. Hamilton, *The Black Preacher in America* (New York: William Morrow and Company, Inc., 1972), p. 88.

36 Schuller, *Ministry In America*, p. xxi.

37 Courtland Milloy, "Black Pastors Seen Losing Authority to Congregations," in *Washington Post*, November 12, 1983, p. 100.

38 *Ibid.*, p. 10.

39 Charles Hamilton in *The Black Preacher in America* indicates that there were approximately 10 million members of Baptist churches in 1972, who were members of the National Baptist Convention, USA, Inc., National Baptist Convention of America and Progressive National Baptist Convention. This does not indicate the number of Blacks in the American Baptist Convention, Southern Baptist Convention, etc. Furthermore, the largest number of Black church members in the United States appears to be the non-hierarchical churches.

40 Norman B. Koller and Joseph D. Retzer, "The Sounds of Silence Revisited," *Sociological Analysis* 41 (Summer 1980), pp. 155-161.

41 *Ibid.*, p. 157.

42 *Ibid.*, p. 157.

43 Marshall C. Grigsby, "The Public Roles of the Black Churches: Education as a Political Problem," *Criterion* 14 (Autumn 1975), p. 9.

44 Wilmore, *Black Religion and Black Radicalism*, pp. 74-75.

Bibliography

BOOKS

Anderson, Gerald H., and Stransky, Thomas F., eds. *Mission Trends No. 4: Liberation Theologies.* New York/Ramsey/Toronto: Paulist Press and Grand Rapids: Wm. B. Eerdmans Publishing Co., 1979.

Assman, Hugo. *Practical Theology of Liberation.* London: Search Press Limited, 1975.

Ayers, Frances O. *The Ministry of the Laity: A Biblical Exposition.* Westminster Press, 1962.

Barrett, William. *Irrational Man: A Study in Existential Philosophy.* Garden City, New York: Doubleday and Co., 1958.

Bennett, Lerone Jr. *Before the Mayflower: A History of the Negro in America.* Chicago: Johnson Publishing Company, Inc, 1962.

Berghe, Pierre L. van den. *Race and Racism: A Comparative Perspective.* New York: John Wiley and Sons, Inc., 1978.

Bobo, Benjamin F., and Osborne, Alfred E., eds. *Emerging Issues in Black Economic Development.* Lexington, Mass.: D. C. Heath Co., 1976.

Bergsman, Joel and Weiner, Howard L., eds. *Urban Problems and Public Policy Choices.* New York: Praeger Publishers, 1975.

Borg, W. R., and Gall, M. D. *Educational Research: An Introduction.* New York, New York: Logman Incorporated, 1979.

Bradbury, Katherine L.; Downs, Anthony; and Small, Kenneth A. *Urban Decline and the Future of American Cities.* Washington: The Brookings Institution, 1982.

Brekke, Milo L.; Strommen, Merton P.; and Williams, Dorothy L. Ten Faces of Ministry. Minneapolis: Augsburg Publishing House, 1979.

Brown, Robert M. *Theology in a New Key: Responding to Liberation Themes.* Philadelphia, Pa.: The Westminster Press, 1978.

Bucy, Ralph D. *The New Laity: Between Church and World.* Waco, Texas: Word, Inc., 1978.

Calvin, John. *On God and Political Duty.* John T. McNeil, ed. Indianapolis: Bobbs-Merrill Educational Publishing, 1980.

Chapmann, Abraham, ed. *Black Voices: An Anthology of Afro-American Literature.* New York and Scarborough, Ontario: The New English Library Limited, 1968.

Childs, John Brown. *The Political Black Minister. A Study in Afro-American Politics and Religion.* Boston, Mass.: G. K. Hall and Co., 1980.

Christian, Robert and Hare, Nathan, eds. *Contemporary Black Thought.* New York: The Bobbs-Merrill Co., Inc., 1973.

Comer, James P., M.D. *Beyond Black and White.* New York: Quadrangle Books, (NYT), 1972.

Cone, James H. *God of the Oppressed.* New York: The Seabury Press, Inc., 1975.

_______. *Liberation: A Black Theology of Liberation.* Philadelphia and New York: J. B. Lippincott Co., 1970.

Council on Interracial Books for Children, Inc. *Fact Sheets on Institutional Racism.* New York: 1984.

Douglass, Frederick. *Narrative of the Life of Frederick Douglass an American Slave.* The Belknap Press of Harvard University Press, 1960.

Dubose, Frances M. *How Churches Grow in an Urban World.* Nashville, Tenn.: Broadman Press, 1978.

Dussel, Enrique. *History of the Theology of Liberation: A Latin American Perspective.* Maryknoll, New York: Obis Books, 1976.

Eliot, T. S. *The Idea of a Christian Society.* New York: Harcourt, Brace and Company, 1940.

Ellison, Ralph. *Invisible Man.* New York/Canada: Random House, 1952.

Fitts, Leroy. *A History of Black Baptists.* Nashville: Broadman Press, 1985.

Franklin, John Hope and Starr, Isidore. *The Negro in the Twentieth Century.* New York: Vantage Books, 1967.

Gilbert, Alan and Gugler, Josef. *Cities, Poverty and Development— Urbanization in the Third World.* Oxford: Oxford University Press, 1982.

Gilder, George. *Wealth and Poverty.* New York: Basic Books, Inc., 1981.

Graham, James J. *The Enemies of the Poor.* New York: Random House, 1970.

Hamilton, Charles V. *The Black Experience in American Politics.* New York: G. P. Putnam's Sons, 1973.

Harvey, David. *Consciousness and the Urban Experience: Studies in the History and Theory of Capitalist Urbanization.* Baltimore, Maryland: The Johns Hopkins University Press, 1985.

Henderson, George. *To Live in Freedom, Human Relations Today and Tomorrow.* Oklahoma: University of Oklahoma, 1972.

Herzog, Frederick. *Liberation Theology: Liberation in the Light of the Fourth Gospel.* New York: The Seabury Press, 1972.

Higginbotham, A. Leon. *In the Matter of Color: Race and the American Legal Process.* New York Oxford University Press. 1971.

Jones, Major J. *Black Awareness: A Theology of Hope.* Nashville and New York: Abingdon Press, 1968.

Jordan, Winthrop D. *White Over Black.* Chapel Hill: The University of North Carolina Press, 1968.

Kasemann, Ernst. *Jesus Means Freedom.* Philadelphia, Pa.: Fortress Press, 1984.

Kerling, Fred N. *Foundations of Behavioral Research.* New York: Holt, Rinehart and Winston, Inc., 1964.

King, Martin Luther, Jr. *Why We Can't Wait.* New York: Harper and Row, 1964.

Kung, Hans. *Does God Exist?* New York: Vintage Books, 1981.

Kuper, Leo. *Race, Class, and Power: Ideology and Revolutionary Change in Plural Societies.* Chicago, Ill.: Aldine Publishing Co., 1975.

Larson, Richard F., Mendenhall, William, and Ott, Lyman. *Statistics: A Tool for the Social Sciences.* North Scituate: Duxbury Press, 1978.

Machiavelli, Niccolo. *The Prince.* Translated by Uigi Ricci. New York: The New American Library of World Literature, Inc., 1952.

Moltmann, Jurgan. *The Crucified God.* New York/Evanston, San Francisco, London: Harper and Row Publishers, 1974.

———. *Man: Christian Anthropology in the Conflicts of the Present.* Philadelphia, Pa.: Fortress Press, 1974.

Morgan, David R. *Managing Urban America.* Mass: Duxbury Press,

1979.

Morton, Grodzins. *The Metropolitan Area As A Racial Problem.* Chicago/Pittsburgh: University of Chicago, and University of Pittsburg, 1958.

Nielsen, Hart M.; Yokley, Raytha L.; Lielsen, Anne K. *The Black Church in America.* New York: London: Basic Books, Inc., 1971.

Oates, Stephen B. *Let the Trumpet Sound: The Life of Martin Luther King, Jr.* New York: Harper and Row Publishers, Inc, 1982.

Paris, Peter. *The Social Teaching of the Black Church.* Philadelphia: Fortress Press, 1985.

Pasquariello, Ronald D.; Shriver, Jr., Donald W.; Geyer, Alan. *Redeeming the City: Theology, Politics and Urban Policy.* New York, N.Y.: Pilgrim Press, 1982.

Peter, Lawrence J., and Hull, Raymond. *The Peter Principle.* New York: William Morrow and Co., Inc., 1969.

Pifer, Alan. *Black Progress: Achievement, Failure and an Uncertain Future.* New York: Carnegie Corporations, 1977.

Raboteau, Albert J. *Slave Religion: The Invisible Institution in the Antebellum South.* New York: Oxford University Press, 1978.

Roberts, J. Deotis. *A Black Political Theology.* Philadelphia, Pa.: The Westminster Press, 1974.

Segal, Ronald. *The Race War.* New York, New York: Bantam Books, 1966.

Schuller, David; Strommen, Merton P.; and Brekke, Milo L., eds. *Ministry In America.* San Francisco: Harper and Row.

______. *Readiness for Ministry—Volume 1 Criteria.* Vandalia, Ohio: ATS, 1975.

Sherman, Richard B. *The Negro and the City.* Englewood Cliffs, New Jersey: Prentice-Hall, Inc., 1970.

Simon, Julian L. *Basic Research Methods in Social Science.* 2nd Edition. New York: Random House, 1978.

Survey Research Center. *Interviewer's Manual.* Rev. ed. Ann Arbor, Michigan: Institute for Social Research, University of Michigan, 1976.

Thomas, George F. *Religious Philosophies of the West.* New York: Charles Scribner and Sons, 1965.

Timms, Duncan. *The Urban Mosaic: Towards a Theory of Residential Differentiation.* Great Britain: Cambridge University Press, 1971.

Torney, George A. *Toward Creative Urban Strategy.* Waco, Texas: Word, Inc., 1970.

Walpole, Ronald E. *Introduction to Statistics.* 3rd ed. New York: Macmillan Publishing Co., Inc., 1982.

Weisberg, H. F., and Bowen, B. D. *An Introduction to Survey Research and Data Analysis.* San Francisco: W. H. Freeman and Company.

Welch, Susan, and Comer, John C. *Quantitative Methods for Public Administration.* Homewood, Ill.: The Dorsey Press, 1983.

Wildavsky. Aaron. *Speaking Truth to Power: The Art and Craft of Policy Analysis.* Boston: Little Brown and Company, 1979.

Wilmore, Gayraud S. *Black Religion and Black Radicalism.* Garden City, N.Y.: Anchor Press/Doubleday, 1973.

Wilson, William J. *Power, Racism and Privilege.* New York, N.Y.: The Macmillan Company, 1973.

Woodson, Carter G. *The History of the Negro Church.*

Young, Pauline V. *Scientific Social Surveys and Research.* Englewood Cliffs, N.J.: Prentice-Hall, Inc., 1966.

ARTICLES

Davis, King E. "The Status of Black Leadership: Implications for Black Followers in the 1980s." *The Journal of Applied Behavioral Sciences* 3 Vol. 1:18, 1982, 309-22.

Grigsby, Marshall C. "The Public Roles of the Black Churches: Education as a Political Problem." *Criterion* 14 (Autumn 1975).

Hadden, Jeffrey K. "Religion and the Construction of Social Problems." *Sociological Analysis* 41(20) (Summer 1980), 99-108.

Hoge, Dean R., Dyble, John E. and Polk, David T. "Influence of Role Preference and Role Clarity on Vocational Commitment of Protestant Ministers." *Sociological Analysis* 41, 1980, 2:155-161.

Kerr, Hugh and Mulder, John M. "New Day—New Laity." Editorial, *Theology Today* 3, Vol. 45 (October 1979), 313-134.

Messer, Donald A. "When the Pastor Enters Politics." *The Christian Minister* (May 1982), 9-12.

Milloy, Courtland. "Black Pastors Seen Losing Authority to Congregation." *The Washington Post*, November 12, 1983.

Nelson, Jill. "Out of Work: The People Behind the Statistics." *Black Enterprise*, May 1982.

Rees, David W. "Goals for the Churches in the 80's." *The Christian Ministry* (January 1980).

Smith, Donald R. "Shared Ministry." *Theology Today* 3 (October 1979), 338-342.

REPORTS AND OTHER SIMILAR SOURCES

"Census Tract and Enumeration District Report—1960 Census of Population and Housing for the Norfolk-Portsmouth Standard Metropolitan Statistical Areas." Southern Virginia Regional Planning Commission, Tidewater Virginia Development Council, Bureau of Business Research, Norfolk College of William and Mary Research Department. *The Virginian Pilot/Ledger Star,* Goodman-Segar-Hogan, January 20, 1961.

Department of City Planning, City of Norfolk. "Address Coding Guide Census Tracts, July 1976.

Division of State Planning and Community Affairs. "Data Summary," Norfolk City, July 1973.

Hammer, Green, Silver Associates. "Norfolk Housing Study," Washington, D.C., April 1970.

Hill, Herbert. "Demographic Change and Racial Ghettos: The Crisis of American Cities." Reprinted from the *Journal of Urban Law.* University of Detroit, Vol. 44, Winter, 1966.

U.S. Bureau of the Census. "Current Population Reports." Series P-20, No. 168. "Negro Population, March 1966." Washington, D.C.: Government Printing Office, 1967.

U.S. Department of Commerce, Bureau of Census. "Current Population Reports." Series P-25, No. 388. "Summary of Demographic Projections." Washington, D.C.: U.S. Government Printing Office, 1968.

Appendices

APPENDIX A

THE QUESTIONNAIRE

INSTRUCTIONS:

Please complete the following questionnaire to the best of your ability. This survey seeks to understand your expectations of a minister in terms of his social and political involvement in the urban community.

1. Please circle the number that corresponds to your denominational affiliation:
   01. African Methodist Episcopal
   02. African Methodist Episcopal Zion
   03. Baptist
   04. Church of God In Christ
   05. Episcopal
   06. Presbyterian
   07. Lutheran
   08. Disciple of Christ

2. SEX: 1. Male   2. Female

3. The following questions address your expectations of a minister. Using the rating scale explained below, please circle the number that corresponds to your feelings:
   1. Highly important
   2. Quite important
   3. Somewhat important
   4. Undesirable
   5. Detrimental
   6. I reject this item; I find it meaningless or irritating.
   7. This criterion does not apply to my denomination or my experience.

1. Actively works for justice in the
   local community.   1 2 3 4 5 6 7
2. Presents a theological basis for
   the mission of the Church.   1 2 3 4 5 6 7
3. Works to improve community
   services to older persons.   1 2 3 4 5 6 7
4. Requests members to hire ex-
   convicts and rehabilitated alco-   1 2 3 4 5 6 7
   holics and drug addicts.
5. Often goes beyond the call of
   duty in working with people.   1 2 3 4 5 6 7
6. Originates activities which con-
   sider youth's interests and   1 2 3 4 5 6 7
   awaken their enthusiasm.
7. Organizes groups to change civil
   laws which seem in the light of   1 2 3 4 5 6 7
   Scripture to be morally wrong.
8. Visits unchurched people to
   share the faith.   1 2 3 4 5 6 7
9. Speaks from the pulpit about
   political issues.   1 2 3 4 5 6 7
10. Locates people to whom he
    might refer individuals not helped 1 2 3 4 5 6 7
    by community agencies.
11. Participates in an effort to
    remove an incompetent or in-   1 2 3 4 5 6 7
    effective official from school,
    church, union, or government.
12. Urges parish to respond to
    critical needs in the world   1 2 3 4 5 6 7
    through sacrificial giving.
13. Insists that clergy should stick
    to religion and not concern them-   1 2 3 4 5 6 7
    selves with social, economic, and
    political questions.
14. Declares a willingness to run for
    public office in the community   1 2 3 4 5 6 7
    (school board, city council, etc.).
15. Priorities in use of time indicate
    the belief that the one and only   1 2 3 4 5 6 7
    way to build an ideal world
    society is to convert everyone

to Christianity.
16. Encourages non-union laborers   1 2 3 4 5 6 7
    to organize.
17. Invites professionals from the   1 2 3 4 5 6 7
    community to participate in con-
    gregational programs or services.
18. Takes an informed position on   1 2 3 4 5 6 7
    controversial issues.
19. Wins the respect and cooperation   1 2 3 4 5 6 7
    of society's outcasts.
20. Works to integrate people of   1 2 3 4 5 6 7
    varying educational, ethnic and
    cultural backgrounds into the
    congregation.
21. Pressures public officials on behalf   1 2 3 4 5 6 7
    of the oppressed.
22. Explores theological issues   1 2 3 4 5 6 7
    underlying current social
    movements.
23. Helps youth identify their gods   1 2 3 4 5 6 7
    and evaluate their adequacies.
24. Alerts members of their need   1 2 3 4 5 6 7
    for learning from Christians in
    other parts of the world.
25. Holds that the church's task of   1 2 3 4 5 6 7
    proclaiming the gospel by
    preaching and teaching over-
    shadows in importance the task
    of helping to eliminate physical
    sufferings of people.
26. Frequently approaches strangers   1 2 3 4 5 6 7
    to ask about the condition of
    their souls.
27. Works to make sure that all   1 2 3 4 5 6 7
    people are free to buy property
    in areas of their choice.
28. Organizes study groups in con-   1 2 3 4 5 6 7
    gregation or community to
    discuss public affairs.
29. Demonstrates understanding of   1 2 3 4 5 6 7
    the influence of social and psy-
    chological forces on people.

30. Urges members to be both   1 2 3 4 5 6 7
    informed and responsive to
    the community needs.
31. Serves on task forces or com-   1 2 3 4 5 6 7
    mittees to improve conditions
    at school or in the neighborhood.
32. Shows concern about liberation   1 2 3 4 5 6 7
    of oppressed people.
33. Uses principles and methods   1 2 3 4 5 6 7
    of social organization for
    political change.
34. Is willing to risk arrest to   1 2 3 4 5 6 7
    protest social wrongs.
35. Actively supports efforts to   1 2 3 4 5 6 7
    improve educational programs
    of the community.
36. Identifies sociological char-   1 2 3 4 5 6 7
    acteristics of congregation
    and community.
37. Stimulates congregation to   1 2 3 4 5 6 7
    new interest and support for
    world missions.
38. Gives pastoral service to all   1 2 3 4 5 6 7
    people with needs.
39. Recommends that the parish   1 2 3 4 5 6 7
    cut off financial support for
    institutions (hospitals, missions,
    etc.) that discriminate against
    minorities.
40. Makes contact with the political 1 2 3 4 5 6 7
    thought and life in the
    community.
41. Seeks to bring everyone to   1 2 3 4 5 6 7
    know God's love in Jesus
    Christ.
42. Organizes action groups in the   1 2 3 4 5 6 7
    congregation to accomplish
    directly some political or
    social goal.
43. Ministers to persons in prisons   1 2 3 4 5 6 7
    and their families, whether
    members of the congregation

or not.
44. Provides community leadership   1 2 3 4 5 6 7
    in ways that awaken trust.
45. Encourages all classes of   1 2 3 4 5 6 7
    people to join the congregation.
46. Works toward racial integra-   1 2 3 4 5 6 7
    tion in the community.
47. Speaks prophetically out of a   1 2 3 4 5 6 7
    conviction that the Church is
    the conscience of humanity.
48. Acquaints self with the history   1 2 3 4 5 6 7
    and aspirations of minority
    groups and other oppressed
    people.
49. Works with different community   1 2 3 4 5 6 7
    factions.
50. Teaches people to reject violence   1 2 3 4 5 6 7
    in words and deeds as not being
    in accordance with the Gospel.
51. Makes individuals aware of   1 2 3 4 5 6 7
    their possible part in causing
    world poverty.
52. Uses authoritative information   1 2 3 4 5 6 7
    and facts to meet racism and
    prejudice in congregation and
    community.
53. Insists that the betterment of   1 2 3 4 5 6 7
    society is not a responsibility
    of the congregation.
54. Acts as though the church should   1 2 3 4 5 6 7
    provide a haven of safety in the
    midst of change.
55. Often expresses doubt about any   1 2 3 4 5 6 7
    good coming from social or
    political change.
56. Does not participate in com-   1 2 3 4 5 6 7
    munity programs for fear of
    alienating members of the
    congregation.

57. What is your predominant racial background?
    1. American Indian
    2. Black (Negro)
    3. Caucasian
    4. Hispanic American
    5. Oriental
    6. Polynesian
    7. Other

58. How much formal education have you had?
    1. Eighth grade or less
    2. Some high school or trade school, but not enough to graduate
    3. High school or trade school graduate
    4. Some college, but not enough to graduate
    5. College graduate
    6. Some graduate or professional school (or seminary), not enough for a Master's degree
    7. Seminary graduate
    8. Master's degree
    9. More graduate or professional school (or seminary) beyond Master's degree
    10. Doctorate

59. Check the figures that come closest to the total income (include estimate of housing and fringe benefits) of all members of your family living at home (before taxes).

    | 1. Under $3,000 | 8. 21,000 - 23,999 |
    | 2. 3,000 - 5,999 | 9. 24,000 - 26,999 |
    | 3. 6,000 - 8,999 | 10. 27,000 - 29,999 |
    | 4. 9,000 - 11,999 | 11. 30,000 - 34,999 |
    | 5. 12,000 - 14,999 | 12. 35,000 - 39,999 |
    | 6. 15,000 - 17,999 | 13. 40,000 - or more |
    | 7. 18,000 - 20,999 | 14. Does not apply |

60. if you are the *main supporter* of your household, answer in this way: Mark the number of the category that is closest to your occupation, based on these U.S. Census Classifications.

    If you are *not* the main supporter of the household in which you are a member, answer in this way: Mark the number of the category that is closest to the occupation of the one who provides the main support of the household.

1. *Clerical and Related Workers*—such as bookkeepers, stenographers, cashiers, mail carriers, shipping clerks, secretaries, ticket agents, telephone operators, etc.
2. *Craft Worker, Blue Collar Worker Supervisor, and Related Workers*—such as tinsmith, bakers, carpenters, masons, shoemakers, electricians, inspectors, cement workers, jewelers, machinists, painters, garage mechanics, etc.
3. *Laborers*—such as garage laborers, car washers, stevedors, lumber workers, teamsters, gardeners, unskilled helpers in construction, manufacturing, farmhands, etc.
4. *Operative and Related Workers*—such as chauffeurs, delivery agents, laundry workers, apprentices, meat cutters, semi-skilled and unskilled employees in manufacturing establishments (bakers, tobacco, textiles, etc.), wholesale and retail workers, mine laborers, bus drivers, motor operators, farm renters, etc.
5. *Private Household Workers*—such as servants, launderers, housekeepers, etc.
6. *Professionals*—such as teachers, editors, dentists, clergy, professors, instructors, doctors, lawyers, nurses, architects, librarians, social workers, etc.
7. *Proprietor, Manager or Official*—such as public official, credit and collection manager, bank officer, floor manager, proprietor, business worker.
8. *Sales Workers*—such as sales workers, insurance and real estate agents and brokers, stock and bond sales agents, newspaper carriers and vendors, demonstrators, etc.
9. *Service Workers, except Domestic*—such as fire, police, barbers, beauticians, janitors, porters, waiters, ushers, practical nurses, etc.
10. *Semi-Professionals, Technical and Similar Workers*—such as funeral directors, photographers, dancers, optometrists, aviators, surveyors, chiropractors, athletes, administrative assistants, accountants, research assistants, teaching assistants, lab technicians, etc.
11. *Farm Owners, Farm Managers*
12. Does not apply

61. What is the approximate size (total membership all ages) of the parish (i.e., congregation) to which you belong or serve?

1. Less than 50
2. 50 - 199
3. 200 - 499
4. 500 - 999
5. 1,000 - 2,499
6. 2,500 - 4,999
7. 5,000 - 9,999
8. 10,000 or over
9. Does not apply

Used by permission of The Association of Theological Schools in the U.S. and Canada.

APPENDIX B

LETTER DESCRIBING THE STUDY TO PASTORS OF SELECTED CHURCHES

June 7, 1984

Dear Reverend,

As part of my graduate studies at Old Dominion University, I am researching the laity's expectations of Ministers in the Black Urban Church. Before commencing the study, I need your help and advice because of your expertise and experience as a pastor.

I would be grateful if you would allow me to speak to you personally about this project in order that a detailed explanation can be provided and specific measures outlined as to how I need your help on gathering the data.

I am scheduling a luncheon meeting on Wednesday, June 20, 1984 at the Hotel Madison in Dolley's Restaurant at twelve o'clock noon (12:00).

I really need your input; so I would be very grateful if you could be present. I promise a delightful lunch and a brief meeting.

Yours In Christ,

James H. Harris

RSVP — Regrets Only by June 15th

APPENDIX C

PROCEDURE FOR ADMINISTERING THE SURVEY

One week prior to the administration of the questionnaire, the pastor will announce that on the following Sunday, he would like for each person to remain after church for approximately fifteen minutes to participate in a survey. The purpose of the advance notice is to minimize the element of surprise and to maximize cooperation. If persons are simply asked to remain after church for the specified time on the same day that the survey is to be administered, the respondent may exemplify a level of resentment or un-coopertiveness that will affect his/her responses. The number of persons in attendance may be affected by the advance announce-ment. Nevertheless at the end of the service on the day that the survey is to be administered, the minister should indicate that the questionnaire will be systematically distributed to every nth person until a sample of fifty persons has been drawn. After actually administering the questionnaire, the persons who did not receive one can be thanked and dismissed. Persons with a questionnaire will then be asked to complete it without collaboration with anyone.

Finally, I will have an assistant to attend the worship service and to distribute the questionnaire, provide pencils and to collect, seal and deliver the completed questionnaires to me on the same day. The assistant will accommodate the pastor in effectuating a smooth administration of the survey.

APPENDIX D

LETTER REITERATING THE ANNOUNCEMENT

July 5, 1984

Dear Reverend,

This is to remind you that the announcement regarding the administration of the questionnaire which will require your members to remain after church for about 15 minutes, should be made on this coming Sunday, July   1984.

Again, I appreciate your assistance in this connection.

The announcement is as follows:

> On next Sunday, July   1984, I would like for each of you to remain after church for approximately fifteen minutes to participate in a survey regarding laity expectations of clergy. Each of you will not be chosen. Those chosen will complete the question-naire while the remainder of you will be dismissed.

Please feel free to elaborate upon the announcement if necessary in order that a maximum level of cooperation might be achieved.

Sincerely,

James H. Harris

JHH/vb

APPENDIX E

TABLES OF STATISTICALLY SIGNIFICANT RELATIONSHIPS BETWEEN INDEPENDENT AND DEPENDENT VARIABLES

TABLE 27

RELATIONSHIP OF DENOMINATION AND RESPONSE TO: ORGANIZES GROUPS TO CHANGE CIVIL LAWS WHICH SEEM IN THE LIGHT OF SCRIPTURE TO BE MORALLY WRONG

	Highly Important	Quite Important	Somewhat Important	Undesirable	Detrimental	Reject Item	Does Not Apply	Row Total
African Methodist Episcopal	1	5	1	0	0	0	0	7
African Methodist Epis. Zion	9	3	7	4	1	1	0	25
Baptist	40	33	26	6	6	5	6	122
Church of God In Christ	27	17	6	7	0	4	6	67
Episcopal	10	12	5	3	0	2	1	33
Presbyterian	7	6	5	0	0	0	0	18
Lutheran	3	3	5	7	3	1	1	23
Disciple of Christ	9	14	11	5	2	0	2	43
TOTALS	105	93	66	32	12	13	16	338

Chi Square = 61.46095   Degrees of Freedom = 42   Significance = 0.0266

TABLE 28

**RELATIONSHIP OF DENOMINATION AND RESPONSE TO:
WORKS TO INTEGRATE PEOPLE OF VARYING EDUCATIONAL
BACKGROUNDS INTO THE CONGREGATION**

	Highly Important	Quite Important	Somewhat Important	Undesirable	Detrimental	Reject Item	Does Not Apply	Row Total
African Methodist Episcopal	2	4	0	0	0	0	1	7
African Methodist Epis. Zion	6	6	6	4	3	0	0	25
Baptist	60	17	26	5	6	3	5	122
Church of God In Christ	35	8	6	3	3	5	7	67
Episcopal	15	12	2	0	1	0	3	33
Presbyterian	11	5	1	0	0	1	0	18
Lutheran	4	6	6	2	3	0	2	23
Disciple of Christ	17	13	9	2	1	1	0	43
TOTALS	150	71	56	16	17	10	18	338

Chi Square = 73.10143   Degrees of Freedom = 42   Significance = 0.0021

116

TABLE 29

**RELATIONSHIP OF DENOMINATION AND RESPONSE TO:
HOLDS THAT THE CHURCH'S TASK OF PROCLAIMING
THE GOSPEL BY PREACHING AND TEACHING OVERSHADOWS
IN IMPORTANCE THE TASK OF HELPING
TO ELIMINATE PHYSICAL SUFFERING OF PEOPLE**

	Highly Important	Quite Important	Somewhat Important	Undesirable	Detrimental	Reject Item	Does Not Apply	Row Total
African Methodist Christ	3	0	2	0	2	0	0	7
African Methodist Epis. Zion	5	2	6	6	1	4	1	25
Baptist	30	17	24	21	14	4	12	122
Church of God In Christ	29	4	11	8	2	3	10	67
Episcopal	11	6	4	5	2	3	2	33
Presbyterian	5	1	2	5	4	1	0	18
Lutheran	3	4	5	3	6	0	2	23
Disciple of Christ	12	10	14	3	3	1	0	43
TOTALS	98	44	68	51	34	16	27	338

Chi Square = 68.82007   Degrees of Freedom = 42   Significance = 0.0056

TABLE 30

**RELATIONSHIP OF EDUCATION AND RESPONSE TO:
PRIORITIES IN USE OF TIME INDICATE THE BELIEF THAT
THE ONE AND ONLY WAY TO BUILD AN IDEAL
WORLD SOCIETY IS TO CONVERT EVERYONE TO CHRISTIANITY**

	Highly Important	Quite Important	Somewhat Important	Undesirable	Detrimental	Reject Item	Does Not Apply	Row Total
Eighth or Less	1	0	4	1	1	1	0	8
Some HS or Trade	15	7	5	3	2	0	4	36
HS or Trade	25	18	10	8	2	6	2	72
Some College	30	15	27	3	10	5	6	96
College Graduate	10	15	14	2	3	5	4	53
Some Grad. or Prof.	9	8	4	8	1	1	0	31
Seminary Graduate	1	0	0	0	0	0	0	1
Master's	4	6	3	4	2	0	1	20
Master's Plus	3	5	2	1	3	0	0	14
Doctorate	0	0	3	1	2	0	1	7
TOTALS	99	74	72	31	26	18	18	338

Chi Square = 77.546112   Degrees of Freedom = 54   Significance = 0.0192

TABLE 31

**RELATIONSHIP OF INCOME AND RESPONSE TO:
PRIORITIES IN USE OF TIME INDICATE THE BELIEF THAT
THE ONE AND ONLY WAY TO BUILD AN IDEAL
WORLD SOCIETY IS TO CONVERT EVERYONE TO CHRISTIANITY**

	Highly Important	Quite Important	Somewhat Important	Undesirable	Detrimental	Reject Item	Does Not Apply	Row Total
Under $3,000	10	4	6	0	0	0	0	20
$3,000-$5,999	2	2	1	0	0	1	3	9
$6,000-$8,999	5	5	1	1	2	1	0	15
$9,000-$11,999	6	6	6	1	1	0	3	23
$12,000-$14,999	9	8	5	8	5	2	1	38
$15,000-$17,999	9	6	8	6	1	1	0	31
$18,000-$20,999	14	5	4	2	0	3	3	30
$21,000-$23,999	6	10	7	4	2	2	0	31
$24,000-$26,999	6	6	7	2	4	3	1	29
$27,000-Up	32	22	28	7	11	5	7	112
TOTALS	99	74	72	31	26	18	18	338

Chi Square = 72.56199   Degrees of Freedom = 54   Significance = 0.0467

TABLE 32

RELATIONSHIP OF OCCUPATION AND RESPONSE TO: WORKS TO INTEGRATE PEOPLE OF VARYING EDUCATIONAL, ETHNIC, AND CULTURAL BACKGROUNDS INTO THE CONGREGATION

	Highly Important	Quite Important	Somewhat Important	Undesirable	Detrimental	Reject Item	Does Not Apply	Row Total
Clerical	19	8	4	2	2	3	1	39
Craft Worker	18	9	10	1	1	0	1	40
Laborer	8	3	7	0	0	1	3	22
Operative	9	5	7	4	1	0	0	26
Household Worker	13	8	5	5	5	3	4	43
Professional	43	19	12	3	3	2	3	85
Manager	8	1	3	0	1	0	1	14
Sales Worker	11	1	1	0	1	1	0	15
Service Worker	4	1	2	0	1	0	3	11
Technical	17	16	5	1	2	0	2	43
TOTALS	150	71	56	16	17	10	18	338

Chi Square = 76.66296   Degrees of Freedom = 54   Significance = 0.0230

TABLE 33

RELATIONSHIP OF OCCUPATION AND RESPONSE TO: ACQUAINTS SELF WITH THE HISTORY AND ASPIRATIONS OF MINORITY GROUPS AND OTHER OPPRESSED PEOPLE

	Highly Important	Quite Important	Somewhat Important	Undesirable	Detrimental	Reject Item	Does Not Apply	Row Total
Clerical	15	5	6	5	3	3	2	39
Craft Worker	13	8	12	4	0	2	1	40
Laborer	11	6	1	0	1	1	2	22
Operative	9	8	6	1	1	1	0	26
Household Worker	13	5	3	11	3	6	2	43
Professional	35	23	17	4	1	0	4	85
Manager	4	7	2	0	1	0	0	14
Sales Worker	4	5	3	1	0	2	0	15
Service Worker	3	2	2	2	1	0	1	11
Technical	13	13	9	6	1	0	1	43
TOTALS	120	82	61	34	12	16	13	338

Chi Square = 73.34665   Degrees of Freedom = 54   Significance = 0.0410

APPENDIX F

THE THREE CORE CLUSTERS AND THEIR PROFILES FROM THE NATIONAL STUDY BY ATS

Reprinted with permission of The Association of Theological Schools in the U.S. and Canada.

TABLE 5-16

Core Cluster 16: Active Concern for the Oppressed
(knowledgeably and earnestly working in behalf of minority and oppressed peoples)

Load	Item No.	Item	Mean
.64	155	Works toward racial integration in the community	1.138
.59	161	Uses authoritative information and facts to meet racism and prejudice in congreation and community	1.326
.54	129	Works to integrate people of varying educational, ethnic, and cultural backgrounds into the congregation	1.502
.54	157	Acquaints self with the history and aspirations of minority groups and other oppressed people	1.168
.45	160	Makes individuals aware of their possible part in causing world poverty	0.163
		* * *	
.45	148	Recommends that the parish cut off financial support for institutions (hospitals, missions, etc.) that discriminate against minorities	–0.166
		Grand mean	1.12

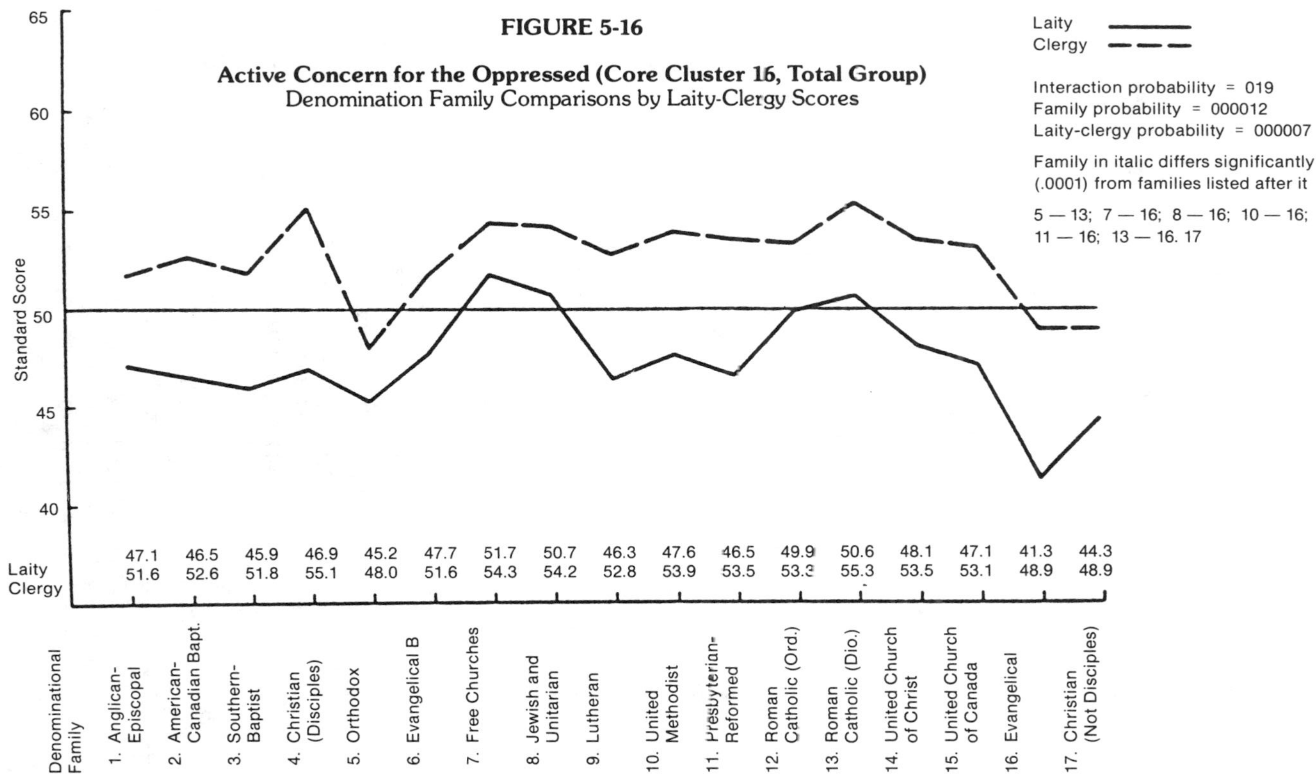

FIGURE 5-16

Active Concern for the Oppressed (Core Cluster 16, Total Group)
Denomination Family Comparisons by Laity-Clergy Scores

TABLE 5-18

Core Cluster 18: Aggressive Political Leadership
(working actively, sometimes using the pressure of community
groups, to protest and change social wrongs)

Load	Item No.	Item	Mean
.65	128	Insists that political struggle is a rightful concern of the Church	0.146
.64	119	Participates in an effort to remove an incompetent or ineffective official from school, church, union, or government	−0.328
.63	117	Speaks from the pulpit about political issues	−0.148
.63	142	Uses principles and methods of social organization for political change	−0.660
.62	115	Organizes groups to change civil laws which seem in light of Scripture to be morally wrong	0.504
.62	124	Encourages nonunion laborers to organize	−1.640
.61	143	Is willing to risk arrest to protest social wrongs	−0.830
.61	136	Works to make sure that all people are free to buy property in areas of their choice	−0.748
.58	130	Pressures public officials on behalf of the oppressed	0.122
.57	137	Organizes study groups in congregation or community to discuss public affairs	0.024
.57	151	Organizes action groups in the congregation or to accomplish directly some political or social goal	−0.432
.51	122	Declares a willingness to run for public office in the community (school board, city council, etc.)	−0.904

* * *

Load	Item No.	Item	Mean
.49	126	Takes an informed position on controversial community issues	1.235
		Grand mean	−0.32

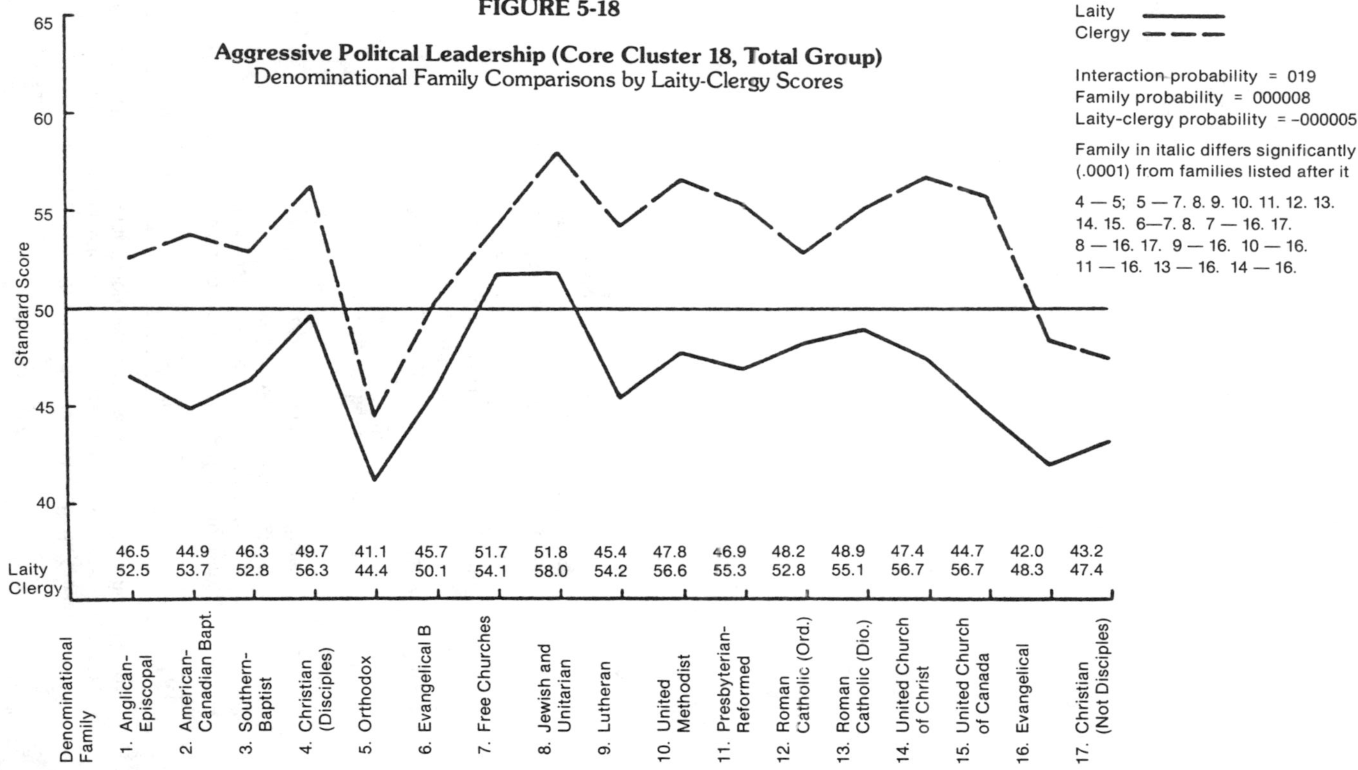

FIGURE 5-18
Aggressive Politcal Leadership (Core Cluster 18, Total Group)
Denominational Family Comparisons by Laity-Clergy Scores
Laity
Clergy
Standard Score
65
60
55
50
45
40
Interaction-probability = 019
Family probability = 000008
Laity-clergy probability = -000005
Family in italic differs significantly
(.0001) from families listed after it
4 — 5; 5 — 7. 8. 9. 10. 11. 12. 13.
14. 15. 6—7. 8. 7 — 16. 17.
8 — 16. 17. 9 — 16. 10 — 16.
11 — 16. 13 — 16. 14 — 16.
Laity   46.5 44.9 46.3 49.7 41.1 45.7 51.7 51.8 45.4 47.8 46.9 48.2 48.9 47.4 44.7 42.0 43.2
Clergy   52.5 53.7 52.8 56.3 44.4 50.1 54.1 58.0 54.2 56.6 55.3 52.8 55.1 56.7 56.7 48.3 47.4
Denominational Family
1. Anglican-Episcopal
2. American-Canadian Bapt.
3. Southern-Baptist
4. Christian (Disciples)
5. Orthodox
6. Evangelical B
7. Free Churches
8. Jewish and Unitarian
9. Lutheran
10. United Methodist
11. Presbyterian-Reformed
12. Roman Catholic (Ord.)
13. Roman Catholic (Dio.)
14. United Church of Christ
15. United Church of Canada
16. Evangelical
17. Christian (Not Disciples)

Core Cluster 19: Precedence Evangelistic Goals
(strong belief that efforts for the betterment of society are of minor
importance by comparison with the evangelization of all humankind)

Load	Item No.	Item	Mean
.67	134	Holds that the church's task of proclaiming the gospel by preaching and teaching overshadows in importance the task of helping to eliminate physical sufferings of people	−0.554
.67	135	Frequently approaches strangers to ask about the condition of their souls	−1.177
.61	123	Priorities in use of time indicate the belief that the one and only way to build an ideal world society is to convert everyone to Christianity	−0.508
.56	121	Insists that clergy should stick to religion and not concern themselves with social, economic, and political questions	−1.178
		Grand mean	−0.94

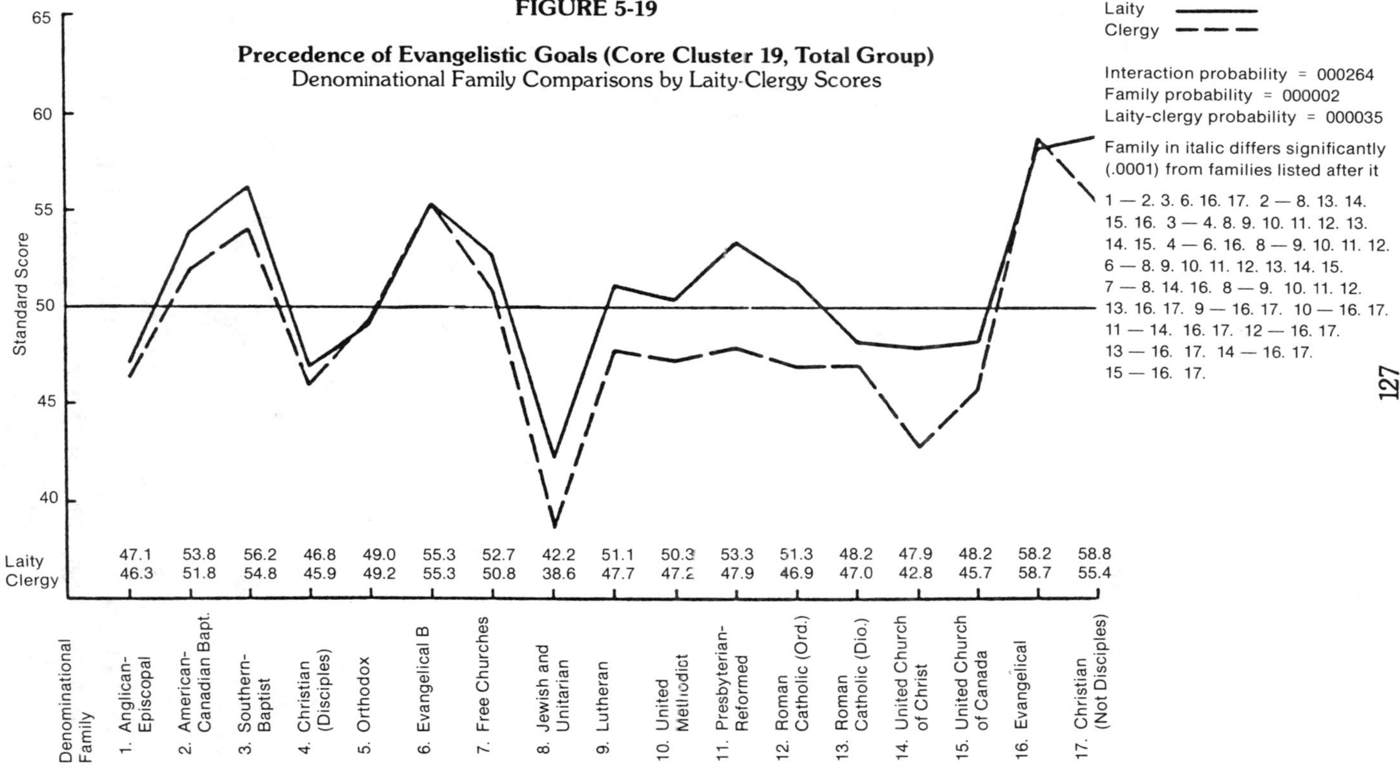

FIGURE 5-19
Precedence of Evangelistic Goals (Core Cluster 19, Total Group)
Denominational Family Comparisons by Laity-Clergy Scores
Laity
Clergy
Standard Score
65
60
55
50
45
40
Interaction probability = 000264
Family probability = 000002
Laity-clergy probability = 000035
Family in italic differs significantly (.0001) from families listed after it
1 — 2. 3. 6. 16. 17. 2 — 8. 13. 14. 15. 16. 3 — 4. 8. 9. 10. 11. 12. 13. 14. 15. 4 — 6. 16. 8 — 9. 10. 11. 12. 6 — 8. 9. 10. 11. 12. 13. 14. 15. 7 — 8. 14. 16. 8 — 9. 10. 11. 12. 13. 16. 17. 9 — 16. 17. 10 — 16. 17. 11 — 14. 16. 17. 12 — 16. 17. 13 — 16. 17. 14 — 16. 17. 15 — 16. 17.
Laity
Clergy
47.1 53.8 56.2 46.8 49.0 55.3 52.7 42.2 51.1 50.3 53.3 51.3 48.2 47.9 48.2 58.2 58.8
46.3 51.8 54.8 45.9 49.2 55.3 50.8 38.6 47.7 47.2 47.9 46.9 47.0 42.8 45.7 58.7 55.4
Denominational Family
1. Anglican-Episcopal
2. American-Canadian Bapt.
3. Southern-Baptist
4. Christian (Disciples)
5. Orthodox
6. Evangelical B
7. Free Churches
8. Jewish and Unitarian
9. Lutheran
10. United Methodist
11. Presbyterian-Reformed
12. Roman Catholic (Ord.)
13. Roman Catholic (Dio.)
14. United Church of Christ
15. United Church of Canada
16. Evangelical
17. Christian (Not Disciples)
127

APPENDIX G

EXAMPLES OF INSTITUTIONAL RACISM REGARDING INCOME, PER CAPITA INCOME, UNEMPLOYMENT AND TYPES OF JOBS HELD BY MINORITIES

Tables 19, 20 and 21, reprinted with permission of "The Council on Interracial Books for Children, Inc." New York, N.Y.

TABLE 19

PER CAPITA INCOME, 1982

White	$9,527
Black	5,360
Hispanic	5,548

SEX, RACE AND HIGH INCOME, 1982

Percent of Persons 14 Years or Older Earning $25,000 or More:

Male White	25.2%	Female White	4.1%
Male Black	10.8%	Female Black	2.5%

TABLE 20

UNEMPLOYMENT

Rates, Race and Age, May 1984

Whites	6.4%
Blacks	15.8%
Hispanic	10.5%
White Teenagers	16.2%
Black Teenagers	44.1%

Source: U.S. News and World Report, 6/11/84

TABLE 20 (Continued)

SEX, RACE AND HIGH INCOME, 1982

The unemployment rates for college graduates were:

White Males	1.6%	White Females	2.4%
Black Males	5.5%	Black Females	3.1%
Hispanic Males	3.8%	Hispanic Females	2.8%

TABLE 21

TYPES OF JOBS

Where Do Minorities Work? 1982

Nationwide Industry	Officials % Managers	% Black Laborers	% Black Service Workers	% Hispanic Officials % Managers	% Hispanic Laborers	% Hispanic Service Workers
Motion Pictures	4.6%	20.3%	10.9%	2.6%	9.7%	5.9%
Communications	7.0%	10.1%	30.0%	2.8%	7.8%	6.7%
Special Trade Contr.	2.1%	25.0%	22.4%	1.9%	13.7%	7.9%
General Bldg. Contractors	1.9%	25.6%	25.3%	2.3%	14.5%	13.0%
Apparel & Textile	4.2%	18.6%	22.3%	3.8%	12.8%	8.9%
Air Transport	3.8%	27.7%	13.8%	1.3%	15.0%	5.9%
Security/ Comm. Broker	3.7%	16.5%	21.3%	3.1%	7.1%	6.0%
Hotels & Lodg. Places	7.9%	23.5%	21.9%	4.9%	27.5%	17.5%
Legal Services	6.5%	39.3%	35.8%	1.8%	32.1%	13.9%
Summary of All Indus.	4.3%	18.7%	21.8%	2.4%	12.5%	8.4%

Source: Equal Employment Opportunity Analysis Reports, 1982.

APPENDIX H

DEFINITION OF TERMS

LAITY   Persons who are non-clergy and constituents of the church.

CLERGY   Persons who are licensed or ordained to the ministry without regard to formal seminary education. One who has responded to the "call."

MINISTRY   Ministry is used here to indicate the function of the person as it relates to his ministerial status such that reference is made to the total realm of involvement of the minister as he/she perceives and practices it within the overall Christian purview. Persons who are ordained or licensed by whatever religious body they represent are said to be in ministry.

MINISTER   To be used here to refer to the pastor of a church body or an ordained, licensed person. Note that a minister is for practical purposes synonymous with clergy. The term pastor, more specifically, implies having charge over a particular church body or congregation.

Index

Activist, 51
Affective approach, 28
AFL-CIO, 20
African, 52
Afro-American, 1
  (See also Black Americans)
Aggressive political leadership, 9,
    13, 14, 16, 29-30, 47
Ambivalence, 51-62
Anxiety, 55-57
Archetype, 39
Aristotle, 40
Association of Theological Schools
  in America, 68, 88
Autonomy, 7
Auxiliary affect, 56

Banfield, Edward, 33
Baptist Church, 7
Black Americans, 1
Black church, 1-9 *f.f.*
Black graduates, 12
Black laity, 2
Black theology, 75-85
Bradbury, Katherine, 23
Brekke, Milo, 67, 86, 91
Brultmann, Rudolph, 78

Calvin, John, 55
Chi-Square, 10, 39, 46
Christianity, 41
Christological, 39
Church of God In Christ, 10
Clusters, 9
Cognitive approach, 28

College, 12
Community, 54
Cone, James H., 76-83
Creativity, 7

Demographics, 11
Demythologizing, 37
Dependent viable, 14
Depression, 24
Dichotomy, 39
Dichotomy (inherent in man), 55
Discrimination, 37, 52
Dualism, 52
DuBois, W.E.B., 62
Duress, 34

Ecclesiology, 45
Ellison, Ralph, 79
Employment, 57-60
Ethiopia, 34
Evangelistic, 39, 43-44
Evers, Medger, 61

Father figure, 60
Fear, 60
    of physical harm, 60-62

Gilder, George, 33
Great Society programs, 59
Grigsby, Marshall, 92
Gutierrez, Gustavo, 75-76

Hamilton, Charles, 91
Hermeneutics (political), 77
Hermeneutical scheme, 78

Heterogeneous, 34
Homilies, 29
Homogeneous, 23

Independent variable, 15, 45
Integration, 33
Jackson, Rev. Jesse, 6
Jefferson, Thomas, 91

Kasemann, Ernst, 77
Kerygmatic, 83
Kierkegaard, Soren, 55
King, Martin Luther, Jr., 21, 61, 85
Koller, Norman, 90

Labor unions, 20
Laity, 9-40
Lasch, Christopher,
Legal duress, 34
Liberation (perspectives on) 75-81
Luther, Martin, 55

Macrocosmic, 47
Malcolm X, 6, 61
Milieu, 54, (social), 59
Moltmann, Jurgen, 76-78
Montgomery Bus Boycott, 19

Narcissism, 55-57
Niebuhr, Reinhold, 55-56
Non-union, 20
Null hypothesis, 46

Ontological significance, 56
Oppressed, active concern for, 9,
    13, 14, 30, 38-39, 44, 47
Oppression, 24, 35

Paradox, 51
Parks, Rosa, 19
Passivity, 66
Peter Principle, 16
Plato, 40
Plotinus, 40
Polemics, 27
Politcal issues, 17-19
Politicism, 51, (political
    perspective), 6, 7
Poverty, 13, 35-36, 66

Precedence (of evangelistic goals),
    9, 43-45
Priestly, 65
Prosser, Gabriel, 6, 92
Prototype/prototypal, 42, 65

Racial homogeneity, 23
Racism, 32
Reagan Administration, 20
Retributions, 7
Retzer, Joseph, 90
Roberts, J. Deotis, 84
Ruether, Rosemary, 76

Scott, Dred Decision, 79
Schuller, David, 67, 86, 91
Segregated, 33
Segregation (residential), 54
Self-determining, 5
Selfishness, 52-54
Social organization, 18
Socio-economic, 16, 46
Southern Christian Leadership
    Conference, 19
Strommen, Merton, 67, 86, 91
Suicide, 24
Suitts, Steve, 12

Theology (liberation and Black),
    75-94
Till, Emmet, 61
Tillich, Paul, 56
Turner, 6, 61, 92

Unemployment, 58-60, 90
United Nations Development
    Program (UNDP), 35
Urban America, 53 *f.f.*
Urban minister, 1-8 *f.f.*

Vessey, Denmark, 6, 92

Walker, Wyatt T., 6
Washington, Joseph R., 66
Wilmore, Gayraud, 91-92

Young, Andrew, 6

About the Author

James H. Harris is Pastor of Mount Pleasant Baptist Church, Norfolk, Virginia. He has served as Adjunct Assistant Professor in the Department of Philosophy at Old Dominion University and Lecturer in Practical Theology for the Evans-Smith Institute sponsored by Virginia Union University and the Baptist General Convention of Virginia. Dr. Harris is a graduate of Virginia State University, Petersburg, Virginia, and holds the Master of Divinity degree from the School of Theology, Virginia Union University. He also holds the M.A. in Humanities and the Ph.D. in Urban Services from Old Dominion University. Dr. Harris is actively involved in Pastoral Ministry, teaching and urban community affairs.